Jonathan Edwards on Evangelism

Jonathan Edwards on Evangelism

Edited

by

CARL J. C. WOLF

WIPF & STOCK · Eugene, Oregon

Wipf and Stock Publishers
199 W 8th Ave, Suite 3
Eugene, OR 97401

Jonathan Edwards on Evangelism
By Edwards, Jonathan and Wolf, Carl J. C.
ISBN 13: 978-1-62564-382-7
Publication date 10/1/2013
Previously published by Wm. B. Eerdmans, 1958

TO

CLARALICE

*whose encouragement is
mellowed with patience*

Preface

Interest in Christianity has grown in our day. Many have expressed the opinion that perhaps we are experiencing another history-making revival. "Evangelism" is in the forefront of denominational programs, and every means of modern communication is being used to tell the gospel story.

The popular interest, of course, centers in personalities; in the men whose voices hold great audiences from pulpit and platform, over radio and television stations. These men are compared and criticized, praised and condemned, supported and opposed. Results are measured by various standards, and conclusions differ.

The student of church history almost certainly will compare today's interest in religion with religious movements in the past, to discover what similarities exist. How does the present development resemble similar events at the turn of the nineteenth century; or The Great Awakening in America's early colonial days? It is even more fascinating to contrast the great personalities of those movements with the leading evangelists of today.

One of the earliest figures in the history of American religious revivals is Jonathan Edwards. Theologians and philosophers, historians and students of literature all acclaim him as one of the great men of the past. Edwards was the outstanding intellectual personality of colonial America, and without a doubt one of the greatest minds that America has ever produced.

A central figure of The Great Awakening, a revival which is remembered for its unusual emotional outbursts,

Edwards is popularly regarded as a preacher of imprecatory sermons. An outstanding example is the famous Enfield sermon with its familiar quote: "The God that holds you over the pit of hell, much as one holds a spider over the fire, is dreadfully provoked; his wrath toward you burns like fire. It is nothing but his hand that keeps you from falling into the fire every moment." It should be remembered, however, that this sermon is typical of the preaching of Edwards' time. Almost every pulpit resounded with warnings about the sufferings of hell. The effort to "scare people into salvation" was the accepted homiletical approach.

The fact is that Edwards was not an emotional preacher and that he usually delivered his sermons almost without gesture, using a quiet but direct manner of delivery. It was inevitable that, from time to time, he should follow the accepted approach, but what is noteworthy about his preaching is that it led to so many conversions. His biographers are generally agreed that this success was due to the remarkable personality of the man and the scholarly content of his messages, rather than the manner of delivery.

In his thinking and preaching and teaching, Edwards is primarily concerned with the sovereignty of God. The Enfield sermon, and similar writings, do not reflect his true genius. He can be seen at his best when he contrasts the greatness and love of God with the littleness of man. His is a God-centered approach, and he has no room for any theological position which hints at a limitation upon the Almighty. Even the most renowned of his writings, *The Freedom of the Will*, can be better understood when one realizes this. It is not a philosophical dissertation or a psychological essay; rather it is a polemic in behalf of Edwards' understanding of God.

Every true revival is accompanied by a theological regeneration. Edwards was not only the preacher of The

Great Awakening, he was also its theologian. One writer goes so far as to call him its "human author," a thought which Edwards himself would certainly have disputed. Edwards is a theologian's theologian, a polemicist par excellence, a biblical preacher of mastery, a practical pastor and philosophical giant, a psychologist before his time. His spirit reflects a rare mingling of systematic theology and personal (mystical) religion. In his diary he wrote: "Resolved: That every man should live to the glory of God. Resolved second: That whether others do this or not, I will." His total writings leave one with the feeling that the sovereignty of God and the love of God really belong together; that Sovereignty is best explained in Almighty Grace. Edwards was a true saint who reconciled within himself what he tried to give to the world. A personal relationship to God is vital, however one may arrive at it; intellect, emotion, and all else are but tools to this end.

Anyone who wishes to study religious revival, to analyze the factors which comprise such a movement, must read this great theologian-evangelist. Edwards' keen insight, his sifting of the facts, his defense of The Great Awakening while admitting its weaknesses — all of these are important to an understanding of revival. Is it possible that in Edwards' teaching we have one of the true secrets of religious revival, namely, the correlation of divine sovereignty and experimental (experiential) faith? His most recent biographer, Perry Miller of Harvard, pictures the man as a genius who was "from an insight into science and psychology so much ahead of his time that our own can hardly be said to have caught up with him."

II

Jonathan Edwards was born in 1703 at Windsor, Connecticut, the son of a minister and the only boy in a family of eleven children. He graduated from Yale with a B.A. degree a short while before he was seventeen. He continued there for two years, preparing for the ministry, and received the M.A. degree.

At twenty-four years of age he became a colleague with his maternal grandfather, the Rev. Solomon Stoddard, in the church at Northampton, Massachusetts. Later, upon Mr. Stoddard's death, Edwards became pastor. It was during the years in this community that he produced the bulk of his writings. At the same time he was faithful to the people of his congregation. His biographers give much credit to his wife, Sarah Pierpont, who kept the home and managed the large family and its affairs so efficiently that Edwards could spend twelve and more hours a day in his study. It was during these years of the Northampton pastorate that The Great Awakening took place, beginning about 1734.

Edwards had been at Northampton more than twenty years when the tragedy of his life occurred — dismissal by the congregation. Mr. Stoddard, during his pastorate, had upheld the Half-Way Covenant, a position which accepted the sacrament of the Lord's Supper as a means of grace in the objective sense. People who at least outwardly lived a good life were urged to participate in the sacrament as a means of leading them to conversion. Edwards had some hesitation about this when he first went to Northampton, but it was not until years later that he developed the conviction that it was wrong, and that he could not continue to uphold the practice with good conscience. He took the stand that the sacrament must be limited to professing Christians. After this his relationship with the congregation became strained. The controversy between himself and the people grew more severe, and finally he was asked to leave.

In 1751 he was installed as a missionary to the Indians.
Whether he ever really was able to adjust to this work,
we do not know, but his ministry there does not seem to
have produced any marked success. It did prove, however, to be a wonderful retreat during which he produced
those two great treatises on *The Will* and *Original Sin.*
Perhaps the recognition which he gained by his writing on
The Will influenced the trustees of New Jersey College
(now Princeton University) to consider him for the pres-
idency of the college and to offer him this position. He
had been president only a short time when, after an inocu-
lation for smallpox, he died in the year 1758.

The volume of material which Jonathan Edwards produced rather staggers the modern reader. Moreover, his
sermons are often repetitious, and the discourses which
took him two and more hours to deliver are not always
suggestive of greatness. But we must discover what he says,
for his originality, intellectual greatness, and penetrating
analyses throw a clear beam of light on the religious movement of today. What this great man said and thought can
help us.

The present digest gives the gist of each of Edwards'
most important writings on evangelism, and it does this
in Edwards' own words. It eliminates much of the repetition which was so characteristic of early eighteenth-century
writings. It is interesting to note here that John Wesley
considered *A Treatise Concerning Religious Affections* so
important that he made an abridgment of it; and this
was eventually printed, although not during Wesley's life-
time.

The writings of Edwards have appeared in every generation. The American Tract Society must have distrib-
uted approximately one million copies of Edwards' various
writings before it ceased to list them among its publications
in 1829. During the last twenty years, several volumes

have been made available which give selections from
Edwards' writings; and very recently some previously unpublished works have appeared. It is hoped that the
present volume will make Edwards' thought available to
those who have neither time nor inclination to read all of
Edwards' writings but who still wish to make the great
man's acquaintance.

NOTES

Taken from *The Works of President Edwards,* in eight
volumes, edited by Samuel Austin and published by
Isaiah Thomas at Worcester, Mass., 1808-1809, First
American Edition, are the following: *A Faithful Narrative
of the Surprising Work of God, Thoughts on the Revival of
Religion, A Treatise Concerning Religious Affections,* the
sermon "Sinners in the Hands of an Angry God," and
the sermon "Reality of Spiritual Light."

Whereas Edwards is generally known for the sermon
"Sinners in the Hands of an Angry God," this sermon was
not preached until the year 1741, after the revival had
been alive for some years. The selection of the sermon
"Reality of Spiritual Light" shows us what Edwards
preached in the year 1734, when the revival actually
began. The *Narrative* appeared in 1737, *Thoughts on Revival* in 1742, and *Religious Affections* in 1746.

The selections from *The Treatise on Grace* and
Directions for Judging of Persons' Experiences were taken
from *Selections from the Unpublished Writings of Jonathan Edwards,* edited with an introduction by Alexander
B. Grossart, Edinburgh, 1865.

Contents

Jonathan Edwards on Evangelism

A Faithful Narrative
of the
Surprising Work of God

A Faithful Narrative of the Surprizing Work of God
in the Conversion of many Hundred Souls in Northampton and the Neighboring Towns and Villages,
in a Letter to the Reverend Dr. Benjamin Colman
of Boston, pastor of the Brattle Street Church.

REVEREND AND HONORED SIR,

Having seen your letter to my honored uncle Williams,
of Hatfield, wherein you inform him of the notice that has
been taken of the late wonderful work of God in this and
some other towns in this county; as also of your desire to
be more perfectly acquainted with it by some of us on the
spot; I would now do it in as just and faithful a manner
as in me lies.

Introductory Statement

The people of the county are as sober, and orderly, and
good sort of people as in any other part of New England;
and I believe they have been preserved the freest by far
of any part of the country from error and variety of sects
and opinions. Our being so far within the land, and at a
distance from seaports, has doubtless been one reason why
we have not been so corrupted with vice as most other
parts. But without question the religion and good order

17

of the country, and their purity in doctrine, has been much owing to the great abilities of my venerable and honored grandfather Stoddard.

The town of Northampton is of about eighty-two years' standing, and has now about two hundred families. In general, so far as I can judge, they are as rational and understanding a people as most I have been acquainted with. Many have been noted for religion, and have been remarkable for their distinct knowledge in things that relate to heart religion and Christian experience.

I am the third minister that has been settled in the town. The Rev. Mr. Eleazar Mather, the first, ordained in July 1669, was blessed with no small success. The Rev. Mr. Stoddard, who succeeded him, was ordained September 1672. He continued in the work of the ministry here near sixty years. He had five harvests, as he called them: the first was about fifty-seven years ago; the second about fifty-three years; the third about forty; the fourth about twenty-four; and the last about eighteen years ago. Some of these were more remarkable than others. But in each, I have heard my grandfather say, the greater part of the young people in town seemed to be mainly concerned for their eternal salvation.

After the last of these came a far more degenerate time (at least among the young people) than ever before. The greater part seemed to be at that time very insensible of the things of religion. Just after my grandfather's death, it seemed to be a time of extraordinary dullness in religion; licentiousness for some years greatly prevailed among the youth of the town. They were addicted to night-walking, and frequenting the tavern, and lewd practices, without any regard to order in the families they belonged to. Family government did too much fail in the town. There had also long prevailed in the town a spirit of contention between two parties, and they were prepared to oppose one another in all public affairs.

But in the two or three years after Mr. Stoddard's death there began to be a sensible amendment of these evils. At the latter end of the year 1733 there appeared a very unusual flexibleness and yielding to advice in our young people. It had been too long their manner to make the evening after the Sabbath, and after our public lecture, to be especially the time of their company-keeping. A sermon was now preached on the Sabbath, before the lecture, to show the evil tendency of this practice; and it was urged on the heads of families to govern their families. But parents found little occasion for the exercise of government in the case; the young people declared themselves convinced by what they heard from the pulpit, and were willing of themselves to comply with counsel.

After this, there began to appear a remarkable religious concern at a little village belonging to the congregation, where a few families were settled, at about three miles distance from the town. At this place a number of persons seemed to be savingly wrought upon. In April 1734 there happened a very sudden and awful death of a young man in the bloom of youth; who, being violently seized with pleurisy, died in two days; which (together with what was preached publicly on that occasion) much affected many young people. This was followed with another death of a young married woman who had been considerably exercised in mind about the salvation of her soul before she was ill; but she seemed to have satisfying evidences of God's saving mercy to her before her death. She died, warning and counselling others. There began evidently to appear more of a religious concern on people's minds.

About this time began the great noise that was in this part of the country about Arminianism. The friends of vital piety trembled for fear of the issue; but it seemed, contrary to their fear, strongly to be overruled for the promoting of religion. Many seemed with much concern what was indeed the way in which they must come to be accepted with God. There were then some things said publicly concerning justification by faith alone. Although great fault was found with meddling with the controversy in the pulpit, it proved a word spoken in season. The people engaged the more earnestly to seek that they might come to be accepted by God.

Then, in the latter part of December, the Spirit of God began to set in, and wonderfully to work amongst us. There were, very suddenly, five or six persons who were, to all appearance, savingly converted. Particularly I was surprised with a young woman who had been one of the greatest company-keepers in town. It appeared to me that God had given her a new heart, truly broken and sanctified. Though the work was glorious, yet I was filled with concern about the effect it might have upon others. I was ready to conclude (although too rashly) that some would be hardened by it in carelessness and looseness of life. But the event was the reverse. God made it the greatest occasion of awakening to others of anything that ever came to pass in the town. Many went to talk with her, concerning what she had met with.

An earnest concern about the great things of religion, and the eternal world became universal in all parts of the town, among all ages. Other discourse than of the things of religion would scarcely be tolerated in any company. They seemed to follow their worldly business more as a part of their duty than from any disposition they had to it. The temptation now seemed to lie on that hand, to neglect worldly affairs too much and to spend too much time in the exercise of religion. But although people did not ordinarily neglect their worldly business, yet there was then the reverse of what commonly is. Religion was with all sorts the great concern.

There was scarcely a single person in the town, either young or old, that was left unconcerned about the things of the eternal world. Those that were loosest and vainest and that had been disposed to think and speak slightly of vital religion, were now generally subject to great awakenings. The work of conversion was carried on in a most astonishing manner. From day to day, for many months together, might be seen evident instances of sinners brought "out of darkness into marvellous light," and delivered "out of a horrible pit, and from the miry clay, and set upon a rock."

This work of God, and the number of true saints multiplied, soon made a glorious alteration in the town; so that in the spring and summer following, A. D. 1735, the town seemed to be full of the presence of God. There were remarkable tokens of God's presence in almost every house. Our public assemblies were beautiful; the congregation was alive in God's service, very earnestly intent on the public worship. In all companies, on whatever occasions persons met together, Christ was to be heard of and seen in the midst of them. And even at weddings, which formerly were merely occasions of mirth and jollity, there was now no discourse of anything but the things of religion, and no appearance of any but spiritual mirth.

When this work of God first appeared, and was so extraordinarily carried on amongst us, others round about us seemed not to know what to make of it. There were many that scoffed at it. Some compared what we called conversion to certain distempers. But it was observable of many that occasionally came amongst us from abroad with disregardful hearts, that what they saw here cured them of such a temper of mind. Many that came to town, on one occasion or other, had their conscience smitten and awakened, and went home with impressions that never wore off till they had hopefully a saving issue. Till at length the same work began evidently to appear and prevail in several other towns in the county.

The people in South Hadley began to be seized with a deep concern about the things of religion; which very soon became universal. About the same time it began to break forth in the west part of Suffield. It next appeared at Sunderland, then in a part of Deerfield, and in the South part of Hadfield; and the work of God has been very great there. There has been also a very general awakening at West Springfield; and in Enfield for a time. For a short time there was also a very general concern at Northfield. In every place God brought saving blessings with him. As what other towns heard of and found in this, was a means of awakening them; so our hearing of such extraordinary propagation did doubtless for a time serve to uphold the work among us.

This remarkable pouring out of the Spirit of God, which thus extended from one end to the other of this county, was not confined to it, but many places in Connecticut partook of the same mercy. Something of this work appeared in several towns in those parts. This flourishing of religion still continues, and has lately much increased. But this shower of divine blessing has been yet more extensive. There was no small degree of it in some part of the Jerseys, as I was informed when I was at New York (in a long journey I took at that time of year for my health) by some people of the Jerseys whom I saw. Especially the Rev. William Tennent, a minister who seemed to have such things much at heart, told me of a very great awakening of many in a place called the Mountains; and of a very considerable revival in another place under the ministry of his brother, the Rev. Mr. Gilbert Tennent; and also at another place under the ministry of a very pious young gentleman, a Dutch minister, whose name, I remember, was Freelinghousen.

This seems to have been a very extraordinary dispensation of Providence: God has in many respects gone beyond his usual way. The work has been extraordinary on account of the universality of it, affecting all sorts, sober and vicious, high and low, rich and poor, wise and unwise. This dispensation has also appeared extraordinary in the numbers of those on whom we have reason to hope it has had a saving effect; also in that the Spirit of God has so much extended not only his awakening, but regenerating influences. It has been a thing heretofore rarely heard of that any were converted past middle age; but now we have ground to think that many such have in this time been savingly changed. The influences of God's Spirit have also been very remarkable on children; and there are very few houses in the whole town into which salvation has not come in one or more instances. There are also several negroes who appear to have been truly born again in the late remarkable season.

I am very sensible how apt many would be to think that I am very fond of making a great many converts, and of magnifying and aggrandizing the matter. For this reason I have forborn to publish an account of this great work of God. But having now a special call to give an account of it, I thought it might be my duty to declare this amazing work, leaving it with God to take care of the credit. I therefore proceed to give an account of the manner of persons being wrought upon.

Description of the Conversions

Persons are first awakened with a sense of their miserable condition by nature, the danger they are in of perishing eternally, and that it is of great importance to them that they speedily escape and get into a better state. Some are more suddenly seized with convictions; others have awakenings that come upon them more gradually. Others that, before this time, had been somewhat religious and concerned for their salvation, have been awakened in a new manner.

These awakenings, when they first seized on persons, have had two effects: one was that they have brought them immediately to quit their sinful practices and dread their former vices; the other that it put them on earnest application to the means of salvation, reading, prayer, meditation, the ordinances of God's house, and private conference. Their cry was: "What shall we do to be saved?" The place of resort was now altered; it was no longer the tavern, but the minister's house, that was thronged; far more than the tavern had been wont to be.

There is a great variety as to the degree of fear and trouble that persons are exercised with before they obtain any comfortable evidences of pardon and acceptance with God. It has been common that the deep concern on persons' minds has had a painful influence on their bodies. Together with those fears, and that exercise of mind which is rational, they have often suffered needless distress of thought. One knows not how to deal with such persons; they turn everything that is said to them the wrong way. There is nothing the devil seems to make so great a handle of as a melancholy humor.

The drift of the Spirit of God in his legal strivings with persons has seemed most evidently to be, to make way for, and to bring to, a conviction of their absolute dependence on his sovereign power and grace; and a universal necessity of a Mediator by leading them more and more to a sense of their wickedness and guiltiness in his sight. When awakenings first begin, their consciences are most exercised about their outward course; but afterwards, are more burdened with a sense of heart sins. When they begin to seek salvation, they are commonly profoundly ignorant of themselves; they are not sensible how little they can do towards bringing themselves to see spiritual things aright. So it appears not to be their own experience only, but the convincing influence of God's Spirit with their experience that attains the effect. Some of those who have not had so deep a conviction of these things before their conversion have, it may be, much more of it afterwards.

There is in nothing a greater difference, in different persons, than with respect to the time of their being under trouble; some but a few days and others for months or years. There were many in this town that had been before this effusion of God's Spirit upon us for years, and some for many years, concerned about their salvation. Though probably they were not thoroughly awakened, yet they were concerned to such a degree as to be very uneasy. Some had never obtained any comfortable evidence of a good estate, who now in this extraordinary time have received light; but many of them were some of the last.

And whatever minister has a like occasion to deal with souls, in a flock under such circumstances, I cannot but think he will soon find himself under necessity, greatly to insist upon it with them that God is under no obligation to show mercy to any natural man whose heart is not turned to God. It appears to me that if I had taught those that came to me under trouble any other doctrine, I should have taken a most direct course utterly to have undone them. I think that I have found no discourses

more remarkably blessed than those in which the doctrine
of God's absolute sovereignty with regard to the salvation
of sinners, and his just liberty with regard to answering
the prayers, or succeeding the pains of mere natural men,
have been insisted on. I have never found so much immediate saving fruit as from Rom. 3:19, "That every mouth
may be stopped."

Commonly persons' minds before this discovery of God's
justice are exceeding restless, and in a kind of struggle
and tumult; but generally, as soon as they have this conviction, it immediately brings their minds to a calm. And
most frequently, though not always, then the pressing
weight upon their spirits is taken away and a general hope
arises that some time or other God will be gracious. That
calm of spirit continues some time before any special and
delightful manifestation is made to the soul of the grace
of God as revealed in the gospel; but very often a sweet
view of a merciful God immediately follows, or in a very
little time.

The way that grace seems sometimes first to appear,
after legal humiliation, is in earnest longings of the soul
after God and Christ; to know God, to love him, to be
humbled before him, and to have communion with Christ
in his benefits. It must needs be confessed that Christ is
not always distinctly thought of in the first sensible act of
grace (though most commonly he is); but sometimes he is
the object of the mind only implicitly. So sometimes dis-
consolate souls amongst us have been revived and brought
to rest in God by a sweet sense given of his grace and
faithfulness, in some special invitation or promise, in
which is no particular mention of Christ, nor is it accompanied with any distinct thought of him in their
minds. Yet it is not received as out of Christ, but as one
of the invitations or promises of God to poor sinners
through his son Jesus. And such persons have afterwards

had clear and distinct discoveries of Christ, accompanied with special acts of faith and love towards him.

It has more frequently been so amongst us that, when persons have first had the gospel for lost sinners discovered to them, they have thought nothing at that time of their being converted. There is wrought in them a holy repose of soul in God through Christ, and a secret disposition to fear and love him: yet they have no imagination that they are now converted. And indeed it appears very plainly in some of them that before their own conversion they had very imperfect ideas of what conversion was. This town is a place where there has always been a great deal of talk of conversion and spiritual experiences; but when people came to be the subject of them themselves, they found themselves much confounded in their notions. And it seems to have been with delight that they have seen themselves thus brought down and become nothing, that free grace and divine power may be exalted in them.

Many continue a long time in a course of gracious exercises and experiences, and do not think themselves to be converted. None knows how long they would continue so, were they not helped by particular instruction. Satan has a vast advantage in such cases to ply them with various temptations which he is not wont to neglect. In such a case persons do very much need a guide to lead them to an understanding of what we are taught in the Word of God of the nature of grace, and to help them apply it to themselves. I have been much blamed by many that I should make it my practice, when I have been satisfied concerning persons' good state, to signify it to them. But let it be noted that what I have undertaken to judge of, has rather been qualifications, and declared experiences, than persons: not but that I have thought it my duty as a pastor to assist and instruct

persons in applying Scripture rules and characters to
their own case.

Conversion is a great and glorious work of God's
power, at once changing the heart, and infusing life into
the dead soul; though that grace that is then implanted
does more gradually display itself in some than others.
But as to fixing on the precise time when they put forth
the very first act of grace, there is a great deal of difference in different persons; in some it seems to be very
discernible when the very time of this was; but others
are now at a loss.   In some converting light is like a
glorious brightness suddenly shining in upon a person;
in many others it has been like the dawning of the day,
when at first but a little light appears, and gradually
increases. And many are, doubtless, ready to date their
conversion wrong.

Persons commonly at first have had many texts of
Scripture brought to their minds, that are exceeding
suitable to their circumstances.   And it seems to me
necessary to suppose that there is an immediate influence
of the Spirit of God oftentimes in bringing texts of
Scripture to mind; not that it is done in a way of immediate revelation without any use of the memory; but
yet there seems to be an immediate influence.   The converting influences of God's Spirit commonly bring an
extraordinary conviction of the reality of the great things of
religion.

Persons after their conversion speak of things of religion as seeming new to them; that preaching is a new
thing; that it seems to them they never heard preaching
before; that the Bible is a new book. Here was a remarkable
instance of an aged woman of above seventy years that had
spent most of her days under Mr. Stoddard's ministry,
who, reading in the New Testament concerning Christ's
suffering for sinners, seemed surprised at what she read.

Many have spoken much of their hearts being drawn out in love to God and Christ. Such persons among us as have been thus distinguished with the most extraordinary discoveries of God, have commonly in no wise appeared with the assuming, and self-conceited, and self-sufficient airs of enthusiasts; but are eminent for a spirit of meekness, modesty, self-diffidence, and a low opinion of themselves. There has been observable in most a great caution lest, in giving an account of their experiences, they should say too much; and many, after they related their experiences, have been greatly afflicted with fears lest they have played the hypocrite and used stronger terms than their case would allow.

There is a vast difference in the degree and also in the particular manner of persons' experiences: some have grace working more sensibly one way, others in another. There is an endless variety in the particular manner and circumstances in which persons are wrought on. But it all seems evidently to be the same work, the same thing done, the same habitual change wrought in the heart; it all tends the same way, and to the same end; and it is plainly the same spirit that breathes and acts in various persons. The work of God has been glorious in its variety; it has the more displayed the manifoldness and unsearchableness of the wisdom of God, and wrought more charity among his people.

Particular Examples

In order to give a clearer idea of the nature and manner of the operations of God's Spirit, I would give account of two particular instances.

The first is an adult person, a young woman whose name was Abigail Hutchinson, who is now dead. She was of a rational, understanding family: there could be nothing in her education that tended to enthusiasm, but rather to the contrary extreme. She was before her conversion, to the observation of her neighbors, of a sober and inoffensive conversation, and was a still, quiet, reserved person. She had long been infirm of body, but her infirmity had never been observed to occasion anything of religious melancholy.

She was first awakened in the winter season, on Monday, by something she heard her brother say of the necessity of being in earnest in seeking regenerating grace, together with the news of the conversion of the young woman whose conversion so generally affected most of the young people here. This news stirred up a spirit of envy in her towards this young woman, whom she thought unworthy of such mercy; but it engaged her in a resolution to obtain the same blessing. Whereupon she began at the beginning of the Bible, intending to read it through. She continued thus until Thursday, when there was a sudden sense of her own sinfulness. Upon which she turned to the New Testament to see if she could find some relief for her distressed soul.

Her distress grew more and more for three days; until (as she said) she saw nothing but blackness of darkness before her. Her sinfulness appeared very awful to her, especially in three things, viz. her original sin, and her sin in murmuring at God's providence in the weakness and afflictions she had been under, and in want of duty to her parents. On Saturday she continued so earnestly in reading the Bible, searching for something to relieve her, till her eyes were so dim she could not know the letters. She thought of those words of Christ wherein he warns us not to be as the heathen that think they shall be heard for their much speaking; which led her to see that she had trusted in her own prayers and religious performances, and now she was put to a non-plus, and knew not which way to turn to seek relief. Her sense of her own exceeding sinfulness continued increasing from Thursday till Monday.

On the Sabbath day she was so ill that her friends thought it not best that she should go to public worship; but when she went to bed on the Sabbath night, she took up a resolution that she would the next morning go to the minister, hoping to find some relief. As she awakened on Monday she wondered at the easiness and calmness she felt in her mind; and then these words came to her: "The blood of Christ cleanses from all sin," which were accompanied with a lively sense of the excellency of Christ and of his sufficiency to satisfy for the sins of the whole world. She had a repetition of the same discoveries of Christ three mornings together; but brighter and brighter each time. On Wednesday her soul was filled with distress for Christless persons, and she felt a strong inclination to go forth to warn sinners.

She had several days together a sweet sense of the excellency and loveliness of Christ in his meekness, which disposed her to be repeating, "Meek and lowly in heart, meek and lowly in heart." Once she told how she thought she saw as much of God as was possible in this life. At the same time she appeared most remote from any high thought of herself, and of her own sufficiency, but expressed a great desire to be instructed.

Her illness increased upon her; and once, after she had spent the greater part of the night in extreme pain, she awakened out of a little sleep with these words in her heart and mouth: "I am willing to spend my life, for Christ's sake!" The latter part of her illness was seated much in her throat so that she could swallow nothing; but when she saw that she could not swallow, she seemed to be perfectly contented without it as if she had no appetite. She was very weak a considerable time before she died; but, says she, "God has showed me that he can make it easy in great pain." She died as a person that went to sleep, June 27, 1735.

It was doubtless owing to her bodily weakness that her nature was so often overcome; but yet the truth was that she had more grace, and greater discoveries of Christ, than the present frail state did well consist with. She was looked upon among us as a very eminent instance of Christian experience; but this is but a very broken and imperfect account I have given of her. Her eminency would much more appear if her experiences were fully related. But there are (blessed be God!) many living instances of much the like nature, and in some things no less extraordinary.

I now proceed to the other instance, that of a little child whose name is Phebe Bartlet. I shall give the account as I took it from the mouths of her parents, whose veracity none that know them doubt.

She was born in March 1731. About the latter end of April, or beginning of May, 1735, she was greatly affected by the talk of her brother, converted a little time before at about eleven years of age. Her parents did not know of it at that time; but after her brother had talked to her, they observed her very earnestly to listen to the advice they gave to the other children. She was observed to retire for secret prayer, and was more frequent in her closet, till at last she was wont to visit it five or six times in a day.

On Thursday, the last day of July, the child being in the closet, its mother heard it speaking aloud, which had never been observed before. Her mother could distinctly hear these words (spoken in her childish manner, but with extraordinary earnestness), "Pray, blessed Lord, give me salvation! I pray, beg, pardon all my sins!" When the child had done praying, she came out of the closet and came and sat by her mother and cried aloud. Her mother asked her several times what the matter was before she would make any answer. Her mother then asked her whether she was afraid God would not give her salvation. "Yes, I am afraid I shall go to hell!" Her mother then endeavored to quiet her, but she continued thus crying and taking on for some time. At length she suddenly ceased crying and began to smile, and presently said, "Mother, the kingdom of heaven is come to me!" After the child had said this she retired again to her closet.

On the Sabbath day she was asked whether she believed in God; she answered, "Yes": and being told that Christ was the Son of God, she said, "I know it." From this time there has appeared a very remarkable abiding change in the child. When she is in the place of worship she is very far from spending her time as children at her age usually do but appears with an attention very extraordinary for such a child. She seems to delight much in hearing religious conversation; and sometimes appears greatly affected and delighted with texts of Scripture that come to her mind. She has often manifested a great concern for the good of other souls; and has been wont many times affectionately to counsel the other children.

The Passing of the Revival

In the former part of this great work of God amongst us, till it got to its height, we seemed to be wonderfully blessed in all respects. Satan seemed to be unusually restrained. Persons that before had been involved in melancholy were waked up out of it, and those with extraordinary temptations seemed wonderfully to be set at liberty. Not only so, but it was the most remarkable time of health that ever I knew since I have been in the town.

In the latter part of May it began to be very sensible that the Spirit of God was gradually withdrawing from us. The first instance was a man's putting an end to his own life. He was of a family that are exceeding prone to the disease of melancholy. About the same time there were two remarkable instances of persons led away with strange, enthusiastic delusions — one at Suffield and another at South Hadley. After these the instances of conversion were rare here in comparison of what they had been before. Religion remained here, and I believe in some other places, the main subject of conversation for several months after this. Yet in the main there was a gradual decline of that general, engaged, lively spirit in religion which had been before.

As to those that have been thought to be converted among us, in this time, they generally seem to be persons that have had an abiding change wrought in them. There is a new sense of the truth; a new kind of inward labor and struggle of soul towards heaven and holiness. Some that before were very rough in temper and manners seem to be remarkably sweetened. I know of no one young person in the town that has returned to former ways of looseness. God has evidently made us a new people.

We are not so pure but that we have great cause to be humbled; nor so religious but that those who watch for our halting may see things in us whence they may take occasion to reproach us and religion. But in the main there has been a great and marvelous work of conversion and sanctification among the people here. And whatever the circumstances and means have been, and though we are so unworthy, yet so hath it pleased God to work! We are evidently a people blessed of the Lord!

Northampton
Nov. 6, 1736

Thoughts on the Revival of Religion

Some Thoughts Concerning the Present Revival of Religion in New England, A. D. 1740

PART I

Shewing that the extraordinary Work *that has of late been going on in this Land, is a glorious work of God.*

The error of those who have had ill thoughts of the great religious operations on the minds of men, that have been carried on of late in New England, seems fundament-ally to lie in three things:

First. In judging of this work *a priori.*

Secondly. In not taking the Holy Scriptures as a whole rule whereby to judge such operations.

Thirdly. In not justly separating and distinguishing the good from the bad.

First: They have greatly erred in the way in which they have gone about to try this work, whether it be of the Spirit of God or no. If we duly consider the matter, it will evidently appear that such a work is not to be judged *a priori*, but *a posteriori*. We are to observe the effect wrought; and if, upon examination, it be found to be agree-able to the Word of God, we are bound to rest in it as God's work. We shall be rebuked for our arrogance if we refuse to do so till God shall explain how or why. Those texts are enough to cause us to forbear in judging of a work of God's Spirit: Isa. 40:13-14, John 3:8. To judge *a priori* is a wrong way of judging any of the works of God. We are not to resolve how or why God brought this or the other effect to pass, before we give him the glory of it. This is too much for the *clay* to take upon it with respect to the Potter. "We know not what is the way of the Spirit, nor how the bones do grow in the womb of her that is with child; even so we know not the works of God who maketh all."

God has not taken that course, nor made use of those means, which men in their wisdom would have thought most advisable. God has wrought like himself, so as to rebuke and chastise the pride of men, Isa. 2:17. God doth thus, in intermingling so many stumbling blocks with this work, agreeable to that prophecy, Zech. 12:7. God has begun at the lower end, and he has made use of the weak and foolish things of the world to carry on his work. Some of the ministers that have been chiefly improved, have not been so high in reputation among their fellows as others; there is reason to think that it has pleased God to make use of their infirmities. A supine carelessness and a vain wordly spirit in a minister of the gospel is the worst madness and distraction in the sight of God.

Secondly: Another foundation error of those that do not acknowledge the divinity of this work, is not taking the Holy Scriptures as a *whole*, and in itself a sufficient rule to judge by. They have half a dozen different rules to make the thing agree to. Those that I am speaking of will make some use of Scripture, so far as they think it serves their turn; but not as a rule sufficient by itself.

(1) Some make philosophy their rule of judging this work. They say, "There is but little sober, solid religion in this work: it is little else but flash and noise." In their philosophy, the affections of the soul are diverse from the will, and not appertaining to the noblest part of the soul.

They acknowledge that a good use may be made of the affections in religion, yet they suppose that the substantial part of religion does not consist in them; they are rather to be looked upon as something accidental in Christianity.

I cannot but think that these gentlemen labor under great mistakes, both in their philosophy and divinity. There are many exercises of the affections that are very flashy and little to be depended on. But it is false philosophy to suppose this to be the case with all exercises of affection in the soul; and false divinity to suppose that religious affections do not appertain to the substance and essence of Christianity. On the contrary, it seems to me that the very life and soul of all true religion consists in them.

All acts of the affections of the soul are in some sense acts of the will, and all acts of the will are acts of the affections. All exercises of the will are in some degree exercises of soul's appetition or aversion; or which is the same thing, of its love or hatred. Therefore all acts of the will are truly acts of the affections; though the exercises of the will do not obtain the name of passions unless the will, either in its aversion or opposition, be exercised in high degree.

All will allow that true virtue or holiness has its seat chiefly in the heart rather than in the head. The things of religion take place in men's hearts no further than they are *affected* with them. The informing of the understanding is all vain, any farther than it *affects* the heart; or which is the same thing, has influence on the *affections*.

Those gentlemen that make light of these raised affections in religion will doubtless allow that true religion, as has its seat in the heart, is capable of very high degrees. By what name will they call these high and vigorous exercises of the will or heart? I suppose that all will allow that there is nothing but solid religion in heaven; that there holiness of heart is raised to an exceeding great height. These things in heaven are not to be cashiered by the name of great heats and transports of the passions. The more eminent the saints are on earth, the more they are like the saints in heaven.

Though there are false affections in religion, there are also true, holy, and solid affections. It is a stumbling to some that religious affections should seem to be so powerful; they are therefore ready to doubt whether it can be of the Spirit of God. But why should a doubt arise? What is represented in Scripture as more powerful, in its effects, than the Spirit of God? Luke 1:35, I Cor. 2:4, Eph. 1:19, 3:7, Col. 1:11, II Thess. 1:11, II Tim. 1:7.

(2) Many are guilty of not taking the Holy Scriptures as a sufficient and whole rule, in that they judge by those things which the Scripture does not give as any signs or marks, viz. the affects that religious exercises and affections of mind have upon the body. The design of Scripture is to teach us divinity, and not physics and anatomy. If Christ had seen it needful to the church's safety, he would have given rules to judge bodily effects; how the pulse should beat under such and such religious exercises of mind; when men should look pale, and when they should shed tears; when they should tremble, etc. But he has not done it because he did not see it to be needful.

The most specious thing that is alleged against these extraordinary effects on the body, is that the body is impaired and health wronged; that it is hard to think that God would impair health. But if it were so pretty commonly, (which I do not suppose it is), yet it is too much for us to determine that God shall never bring an outward calamity, in bestowing a vastly greater spiritual and eternal good. Jacob, in wrestling with God, at the same time that he received the blessing from God, suffered outward calamity. God impaired his body so that he never got over it as long as he lived. Yet this is not mentioned as if it were any diminution of the great mercy of God.

But, some say, the operations of the Spirit of God are of a benign nature; nothing is of a more kind influence on human nature. But however kind to human nature the influences of the Spirit of God are, yet divine and eternal things, as they may be discovered, would overpower the nature of man in its present weak state. If God did discover but a little of that which is seen by the saints and angels of heaven, our frail natures would sink under it; e. g., Dan. 10:6-8, Hab. 3:16; the psalmist also speaks of an effect I have often seen on persons, Psa. 119:131. We cannot determine that God never shall give any person so much of a discovery of himself, not only as to weaken their bodies, but to take away their lives. It is supposed by very learned and judicious divines that Moses' life was taken after this manner. As I said before, it is too much for us to determine that God will not bring an outward calamity in bestowing spiritual and eternal blessings. God is pleased sometimes, in dealing forth spiritual blessings to his people, to exceed the capacity of the vessel.

(3) Another thing that some make their rule to judge of this work by, instead of the Holy Scriptures, is history. They err two ways.

(a) If there be any thing new and extraordinary in the circumstances of this work, that was not observed in former times, that is a rule with them to reject this as not the work of God. Herein they limit God where he has not limited himself. Besides those things in this work, that have been chiefly complained of as new, are not so new as has been generally imagined. They are things as have been found and well approved of in the church of God before, from time to time. Yea, such extraordinary external effects of inward impressions have not only been found here and there in a single person, but there have been times wherein many have been thus affected. Such effects have appeared in congregations, in many at once. So it was in the year 1625, in the west of Scotland, in a time of great outpouring in the Spirit of God, that they fell down and were carried out of the church, who afterwards proved most solid and lively Christians. I have also been credibly informed that it was a common thing, when the famous Mrs. John Rogers of Dedham in England was preaching, for some of his hearers to cry out.

(b) Another way that some err, in making history their rule, is in comparing some external, accidental circumstances of this work with what has appeared sometimes in enthusiasts; and as they find an agreement in some such thing, so they reject the whole work, concluding it to be enthusiasm.

(4) Some make their own experience the rule, and reject such and such things as are now professed and experienced, because they never felt them themselves. It is to be feared many good men have been guilty of this error; which yet does not make it less unreasonable. They are guilty of casting a great reflection upon the understanding of the Most High.

Thirdly: Another foundation error of those that reject this work is very unjustly judging of the whole by a part. They look for more in men that are divinely influenced than is justly to be expected from them for that reason, in this imperfect state, where so much blindness and corruption remain in the best. The great weakness of the bigger part of mankind, in any affair that is new and uncommon, appears in not distinguishing but either approving or condemning all in the lump. They that highly approve of the affair in general, cannot bear to have anything at all found fault with; on the other hand, those that fasten upon some things in the affair that appear very disagreeable to them, at once reject the whole.

It surely cannot be wondered at by considerate persons, that at a time when multitudes all over the land have their affections greatly moved, that great numbers should run into many errors with respect to their duty, and consequently into many acts and practices that are imprudent and irregular. A high degree of love to God may accidentally move a person to that which is very wrong, and contrary to the mind and will of God. For a high degree of love to God will strongly move a person to do that which he believes to be agreeable to God's will. If he be mistaken, then his love will accidentally, but strongly, incline him to that which is indeed very contrary to the will of God. True disciples of Christ may have a great deal of false zeal, such as the disciples had of old when they would have fire called for from heaven. Men, even in those very things wherein they are influenced by a truly pious principle, yet, through error and want of due consideration and caution, may be very rash with their zeal.

A great deal of darkness mixed with light, and evil with good, is always to be expected in the beginning of something very extraordinary. The weakness of human nature has always, in times of great revival of religion, run to extremes; and especially in three things, enthusiasm, superstition, and intemperate zeal. So it appeared in the time of the reformation; and also in the days of the apostles. Many, as ecclesiastical history informs us, fell off into the most wild enthusiasm and extravagant notions of spirituality. And how much did vain jangling and disputing prevail through undue heat of spirit, under the name of religion, II Tim. 2:16; 4:4, 5; Titus 3:9! And though some of the apostles lived long to settle things, yet presently after they were dead, the Christian church ran into many superstitions and childish notions, and in some respects into a great severity in their zeal.

If we look over this affair and seriously weigh it in its circumstances, it may easily be accounted for that many have run into just such errors as they have. Some that have been improved as great instruments to promote this work have been very young. They have not had the advantage of age and experience, and have had but little opportunity to study divinity or to converse with aged experienced Christians. How natural it is for such to fall into many errors. Why should it be thought strange that those, that scarce ever heard of any such thing as an outpouring of the Spirit of God before, do not know how to behave themselves in such a new and strange state of things? If they be not persons of more than common discretion, it is a wonder if they do not things that are irregular.

Censuring others is the worst disease with which this affair has been attended: but yet such a time as this is indeed a time of great temptation to this sinful error.

Thus I think the errors and irregularities that attend this work may be accounted for, from the consideration of the infirmity and weakness and common corruption of mankind. And it is very analogous to the manner of God's dealing with his people to permit a great deal of error; for by man's exceeding weakness appearing in the beginning of it, it is evident that God does not lay the foundation of it in man's strength of wisdom. We need not wonder at the errors if we look at the hand of men that are guilty of them and the hand of God in permitting them. So neither shall we see cause to wonder at them, if we consider them with regard to the hand that Satan has in them. For as the work is much greater than any other outpouring of the Spirit that ever has been in New England, so no wonder that the devil exerts himself more vigorously against it, and does more powerfully endeavor to tempt and mislead those that are the subjects of it or the promoters of it.

Whatever imprudences there have been, and whatever sinful irregularities; whatever vehemence of the passions, and heats of the imagination, transports and ecstasies; and whatever error in judgment, and indiscreet zeal; and whatever outcries, and faintings, and agitations of the body; yet it is manifest and notorious that there has been of late a very uncommon influence upon the minds of a very great part of the inhabitants of New England. That has been attended with the following effects, viz. a great increase of seriousness, and sober consideration of the things of the eternal world; a disposition to hearken to anything that is said of things of this nature, with attention; a disposition to treat matters of religion with solemnity; and to attend all external duties of religion in a more solemn and decent manner. Through the greater part of New England the Holy Bible is in much greater esteem and use than it used to be. The Lord's day is more religiously and strictly observed. It is astonishing to see the alteration that is in some towns, where before was but little appearance of religion.

Now if such things are enthusiasm, and the fruits of a distempered brain, let my brain be evermore possessed of that happy distemper! If this be distraction, I pray God that the world of mankind may be all seized with this benign, meek, beneficent, beautiful, glorious distraction! If agitation of body were found in the French prophets, and ten thousand prophets more, it is little to their purpose who bring it as an objection against such a work as this, unless their purpose be to disprove the whole of the

Christian religion. Though there are some instances of great affections in which there has been a great mixture of nature with grace, and in some a sad degeneration of religious affections, yet there is that uniformity observable, that it is easy to be seen that it is the same Spirit from whence the work in all parts of the land has originated.

Those that are waiting for the fruits in order to determine whether this be the work of God or no, would do well to consider two things: 1. What they are waiting for: whether it be not this, to have this wonderful religious influence that is on the minds of people over and past, and then to see how they will behave themselves. That is, they are waiting to have persons sicken and lose their strength, that they may see whether they will then behave themselves like healthy strong men. 2. They would do well to consider how long they will wait to see the good fruit of this work, before they will determine in favor of it. Is not their waiting unlimited? Cannot God work on the hearts of a people after such a manner, as to show his hand so plainly, as reasonably to expect it should be acknowledged in a year and a half, or two years' time? Surely it is unreasonable that our demands should be unlimited and our waiting without any bounds.

I am bold to say that the work of God in the conversion of one soul is a more glorious work than the creation of the whole material universe. And it is a work above all others glorious, as it concerns the happiness of mankind.

The work is also exceeding glorious in the high attainments of Christians, in the extraordinary degrees of light, love, and spiritual joy that God has bestowed upon great multitudes. In this respect also the land in all parts has abounded with such instances, any one of which if they had happened formerly would have been thought worthy to be taken notice of by God's people. The New Jerusalem in this respect has begun to come down from heaven, and perhaps never were more prelibations of heaven's glory given upon earth. How unreasonable it is that we should be backward to acknowledge the glory of what God has done.

PART II

Shewing the Obligations that all are under to acknowledge, rejoice in, and promote this Work; *and the great Danger of the contrary.*

There are many things in the Word of God that show that when God remarkably appears in any great work for his church and against his enemies, it is a most dangerous thing, and highly provoking to God, to be slow and backward to acknowledge and honor God in the work. Christ's people are in Scripture represented as his army; he is the captain of the host of the Lord, Joshua 5:13-15. He is the captain of his people's salvation; and therefore it may well be highly resented if they do not resort to him when he orders his banner to be displayed. At a time when God manifests himself in such a great work for his church, there is no such thing as being neuters; there is a necessity of being either for or against the King that then gloriously appears. So it always is when God, in any great dispensation of his providence, does remarkably set his King on his holy hill of Zion. So it was when Christ came down from heaven in his incarnation; there was no such thing as being neuters, Matt. 12:30.

God hath had it much on his heart from all eternity to glorify his dear and only begotten Son; and there are some special seasons that he appoints to that end. These times are times of remarkable pouring out of his Spirit to advance his kingdom. Those that at such a time do not kiss the Son, as he then manifests himself, expose themselves to *perish from the way,* and to be *dashed in pieces with a rod of iron.* It is a time when he remarkably fulfils Isa. 28:16. The two apostles Peter and Paul, (I Pet. 2:6-8, Rom. 9:33), join with that prophecy, Isa. 8:14, 15. Christ is a foundation and a sanctuary for some; he is a stone of stumbling and rock of offense to others.

It is not unlikely that this work of God's Spirit is the dawning, or at least the prelude, of that glorious work of God so often foretold in Scripture, which in the progress and issue of it shall renew the world of mankind. If we consider how long since the things foretold have been accomplished; how long this event has been expected by the church of God; and what the state of things now is in the world of mankind, we cannot but reasonably think otherwise than that the beginning of this great work of God must be near. And there are many things that make it probable that this work will begin in America. It is signified that it shall begin in some very remote part of the world, Isa. 60:9. This new world is probaby now discovered that the new and most glorious state of God's church on earth might commence there; that God might begin a new world in a spiritual respect. God has already put that honor upon the other continent that Christ was born there literally, and there made the *purchase of redemption;* so, as Providence observes a kind of equal distribution of things, it is not unlikely that the great spiritual birth of Christ, and the *application of redemption,* is to begin in this.

It is agreeable to God's manner, when he accomplishes any glorious work in the world, to begin where his church had not been till then, that the power of God might be more conspicuous; that the work might appear to be entirely God's, and more manifestly a creation out of nothing, agreeably to Hos. 1:10, as Isa. 32:15, 41:18, and many other parallel Scriptures. There are several things that seem to me to argue that when the Sun of Righteousness comes to rise, the sun shall rise in the west; as God caused the sun to go from the west to the east when Hezekiah was healed, and God promised to do such great things for his church, to deliver it out of the hand of the king of Assyria by that mighty slaughter by the angel.

If these things are so, it gives us more abundant reason to hope that what is now seen in America, and especially in New England, may prove the dawn of that glorious day. The very uncommon and wonderful circumstances of this work seem to me strongly to argue that God intends it as the beginning of some thing vastly greater.

I have thus insisted it behooves us to encourage and promote this work. It is very dangerous for God's professing people to lie still, and not to come to the help of the Lord, whenever he remarkably pours out his Spirit. This is the proper time of actual redemption, Isa. 65:17, 18; 66:12; Rev. 21:1.

The great danger of not appearing openly to acknowledge, rejoice in, and promote that great work of God, in bringing in that glorious harvest, is represented in Zech. 14:16-19, "Whoso will not come up of all the families of the earth unto Jerusalem to worship the King, the Lord of hosts, upon them shall be no rain, etc." It is threatened that those who shall not come to keep this feast (Tabernacles), i.e., that shall not acknowledge God's glorious works, and praise his name, but should stand at a distance as unbelieving and disaffected, they shall have no share in that shower of divine blessing. But God would give them over to hardness of heart and blindness of mind.

The curse is yet more awful against such as shall appear opposers at that time, vs. 12, "And this shall be the plague wherewith the Lord shall smite the people that have fought against Jerusalem; etc." The great danger of not joining God's people at that day is also represented in Isa. 60:12, "For the nation and kingdom that will not serve thee shall perish."

Most of the great temporal deliverances that were wrought for Israel of old were typical of the great spiritual works of God for the salvation of men's souls, and the deliverance of his church. So when God wrought that great work of bringing the children of Israel out of Egypt, how highly did God resent it when the Amalekites appeared as opposers in that affair! That was a glorious work of God when he delivered them from the Canaanites by the hand of Deborah and Barak, Judg. 5:20, or in the victory that was obtained by Gideon over the Midianites and Amalekites. This was a type of the victory of Christ and his church over his enemies by the pouring out of the Spirit. The return of the Ark of God to dwell in Zion, after it had been long absent in the land of the Philistines and Kirjathearim, did livelily represent the return of God to a professing people, in the spiritual tokens of his presence after long absence from them; as well as the Ark's ascending up into a mountain typified Christ's ascension into heaven. Let us take heed that we be not like the son of the bondwoman, that was born after the flesh, that persecuted him that was born after the Spirit; lest we should be cast out of the family of Abraham, as he was. That affair contained spiritual mysteries and was typical of things that come to pass in these days of the gospel, Gal. 4:22-31. And that we may be warned not to continue doubting, let us consider the example of the unbelieving lord of Samaria, who could not believe a work of God to be accomplished so suddenly as the prophet Elisha fore-told, II Kings 7.

But above all the others is God's eye upon ministers of the gospel, as expecting of them that they should arise and acknowledge and honor him in such a work as this, and do their utmost to encourage and promote it. It is expected of them, above all others, that they should have understanding of the times; for it is their business to acquaint themselves with things pertaining to the kingdom of God, and to teach and enlighten others in things of this nature. It is God's revealed will that whenever that glorious revival of religion and reformation of the world, so often spoken of in his Word, is accomplished, it should be principally by the labors of his ministers. How heinous will it be in the sight of God, if when a work of that nature is begun, we appear unbelieving, slow, backward, and disaffected! There were no sort of persons among the Jews treated with such manifestations of God's displeasure for not acknowledging Christ, and the work of his Spirit, in the days of Christ and his apostles, as the ministers of religion; see how Christ deals with them in the twenty-third chapter of Matthew.

If ministers preach never so good doctrine and are never so laborious in their work, yet, if they show to their people that they are doubtful and suspicious of this work, they will be very likely to do their people a great deal more hurt than good. Besides, their minister's opinion will not only beget in them a suspicion of the work they hear of abroad, but it will also tend to create a suspicion of everything of like nature that shall appear among themselves. We that are ministers need to take heed what we do. If we are very silent about the work, or seem to avoid speaking of it in our conversation, it will and justly may be interpreted by our people that we are suspicious of it.

And this will tend to raise the same suspicions in them. "Woe unto you, for you shut up the kingdom of heaven; for ye neither go in yourselves, neither suffer ye them that are entering to go in," Matt. 23:13. Ministers should specially take heed of a spirit of envy toward other ministers that God is pleased to make more use of to carry on this work than they.

It is our wisest and best way, fully and without reluctance, to bow to the great God in this work, and to be entirely resigned to him with respect to the manner in which he carries on, and the instruments he is pleased to make use of, and not sullenly refuse to acknowledge this work because we have not had so great a hand in it as others. When God comes to accomplish any great work for his church, he always fulfills that Scripture, Isa 2:17, "And the loftiness of man shall be bowed down, and the haughtiness of men shall be made low, and the Lord alone shall be exalted in that day." Not only magistrates and ministers, but every living soul is now obliged to acknowledge God in this work and put his hand to promote it.

All sorts of persons throughout the whole congregation of Israel, great and small, rich and poor, men and women, helped to build the Tabernacle in the wilderness; some in one way, others in another; each according to his capacity, Ex. 35:20ff. Thus it ought to be in this day of building the tabernacle of God. Whatever errors many zealous persons have run into, yet if the work, in the substance of it, be the work of God, then it is a joyful day indeed; it is so in heaven, and ought to be so among God's people on earth; especially in that part of the earth where this glorious work is carried on.

PART III

Shewing in many Instances wherein the Subjects, or Zealous Promoters of this Work, *have been injuriously blamed.*

This work, that has lately been carried on in the land, is the work of God. Its beginning has not been of man's power or device, and its being carried on depends not on our strength or wisdom. But God expects of all that they should use their utmost endeavors to promote it. Yet at the same time, in our endeavors to promote this work, we ought to use the utmost caution. A great affair should be managed with prudence. We had need always to stand on our watch and not be ignorant of the devices of our enemies.

I would take notice wherein fault has been found with the conduct of those that have appeared to be the subjects of it, or have been zealous to promote it, beyond just cause.

First: One thing that has been complained of, is ministers addressing themselves to the affections of their hearers rather than to their understandings, and striving to raise their passions in voice and gesture rather than by clear reasoning. It is objected that the affections are moved without a proportionable enlightening of the understanding.

I am far from thinking that it is not profitable for ministers in their preaching to explain clearly the doctrines of religion; and it is very probable that these things have been too much neglected by many ministers. Yet the objection of affections raised without enlightening the understanding is in a great measure built on a mistake. The thing to be inquired is whether the apprehensions of divine things raised in people's minds by these affectionate preachers be apprehensions agreeable to truth, or whether they are mistakes. If the former, then the affections are raised as they should be, viz., by informing the mind or conveying light to the understanding. An appearance of affection and earnestness in the manner of delivery, if it be agreeable to the nature of the subject, and be not beyond a proportion of its importance, and there be no appearance of its being feigned or forced, has much the greater tendency to beget true ideas in the minds of the hearers.

I know it has long been fashionable to despise a very earnest and pathetical way of preaching; and they only have been valued as preachers that have shown the greatest extent of learning, strength of reason, and correctness of language. But I humbly conceive it has been for want of duly considering human nature that such preaching has been thought to have the greatest tendency to answer the ends of preaching. Clearness, strength of reason, and method are needful, and not to be neglected, yet an increase in speculative knowledge in divinity is not what is so much needed by our people as something else. Men may abound in this sort of light and have no heat. How much has there been of this sort of knowledge in the Christian world in this age? Was there ever an age wherein penetration of reason, extent of learning, exactness of distinction, correctness of style, and clearness of expression did so abound? And yet was there ever an age wherein there has been so little sense of the evil of sin, so little love to God, heavenly-mindedness, and holiness of life among the professors of true religion? Our people do not so much need to have their heads stored as to have their hearts touched, Isa. 58:1; 40:2, 3, 6; 61:1-2; 27:13; Jer. 2:2; Jonah 1:2; John 7:37. And it is worthy to be noted that the word commonly used in the New Testament, that we translate *preach*, signifies to *proclaim aloud like a crier*.

Second: Another thing that some ministers have been blamed for is speaking terror to them that are already

under great terrors instead of comforting them. If ministers, in such a case, terrify persons with that which is not
true, or affright them by representing their case worse than
it is, they are to be condemned; but if they terrify them
only by holding forth more light to them, more of the truth
of their case, they are justified. Why should we be afraid
to let persons that are in an infinitely miserable condition
know the truth or bring them into the light, for fear it
should terrify them? To blame a minister for thus declar-
ing the truth is like blaming a surgeon because when he
has begun to thrust in his lance, whereby he had already
put his patient to great pain, and he shrinks and cries out
with anguish, he is so cruel that he will not stay his hand
but goes on to thrust it in further until he comes to the
core of the wound.

Indeed something else beside terror is to be preached to
them whose consciences are awakened. The gospel is to
be preached to them. They are to be told there is a Saviour
provided, who has shed his precious blood for sinners, that
stands ready to receive them if they will heartily embrace
him. But this is to induce them to escape from the misery
of the condition they are now in. Truth is never more
reasonable than at such a time when Christ is beginning to
open the eyes of the conscience.

I know of but one case wherein truth ought to be withheld from sinners in distress of conscience, and that is the
case of melancholy. It is not because the truth tends to
do them hurt, but because if we speak the truth to them,
sometimes they will be deceived and led into error by it
through that strange disposition there is in them to take
things wrong. But the most awful truths of God's Word
ought not to be withheld from public congregations because some such melancholic persons may be in them.

Third: A great deal has been said against having so frequent religious meetings and spending so much time in
religion. Indeed, there are none of the externals of religion
but what are capable of excess. I believe it is true that of
late we have abounded in religious meetings, and there
has not been a proportionate increase of zeal for deeds of
charity. Yet it appears to me that this objection has been in
general groundless.

Persons ought not to neglect their particular callings.
Worldly business must be done. Yet it is to the honor of
God that a people should be much in the outward acts of
religion; especially when God appears unusually present
in wonderful works of power and mercy. It was so with
the Christian church in Jerusalem, Acts 2:46; and so at
Ephesus, Acts 19:8-10.

Besides, if the matter be justly considered, I believe it
will be found that no time has been lost from temporal affairs by the late revival of religion, but rather time gained.
More time has been saved from frolicking and tavern haunt-
ing that has lately been spent in religion. There is much
more outcry made against this extraordinary religion than
was before against so much time spent in tavern-haunting,
and other things, which wasted both time and substance,
and injured moral virtue.

Fourth: Ministers have been blamed for making much
of outcries, faintings, and other bodily effects; speaking
of them as tokens of the presence of God, and arguments
of the success of preaching.

I would observe, in the *first* place, that there are many
things charged on ministers that they are not guilty of.
Some would have it that they speak of these things as
certain evidences of a work of the Spirit of God. And some
are charged with making these things essential, supposing
that persons cannot be converted without them. It seems

to me they are not to be blamed. To rejoice that the work of God is carried on calmly, without much ado, is in effect to rejoice that there is not so much of the influence of God's Spirit. For though the degree of influence of the Spirit of God on *particular persons* is by no means to be judged by the degree of external appearances, because of the different constitution, tempers, and circumstances of men; yet if there be a very powerful influence of the Spirit of God on a mixed multitude, it will cause some way or other a great visible commotion. Though persons ought to take heed that they do not make much ado without necessity, yet the unavoidable manifestations of strong religious affections are found by experience to have an excellent and durable effect, Zech. 9:15-16.

Fifth: Another thing that gives great disgust to many is the disposition that persons show, under great affections, to speak so much, and with such earnestness to be setting forth the greatness of divine things; and to be so passionately warning others.

Concerning which I would say that I am far from thinking that such a disposition should be wholly without any limits or regulation; and I believe some have erred in setting no bounds, and indulging and encouraging this disposition without any kind of restraint or direction. Yet it seems to me that such a disposition in general is what both reason and Scripture will justify.

Sixth: Many have disliked the religious meetings of children, to read and pray together, and perform religious exercises by themselves. What is objected is children's want of that knowledge and discretion that is requisite to a decent and profitable management of religious exercises. The objection is not sufficient. Children are capable of the influences of the Spirit of God; and if they are inclined by a religious disposition to improve their society with one another in a religious manner, and to religious purposes, who should forbid them? If they have not discretion to observe method in their religious performances, or to speak sense in all that they say in prayer, they may notwithstanding have a good meaning, and God understands them. There is not so much difference before God between children and grown persons as we are ready to imagine. We that are grown have defects in our prayers that are a thousand times worse in the sight of God. If children appear to be really moved by a religious disposition, and not merely from a childish affectation of imitating grown persons, they ought by no means to be discouraged, Matt. 21:15-16.

PART IV

Shewing what things are to be corrected or avoided in promoting this Work, *or in our behaviour under it.*

Many that are zealous for this glorious work of God are heartily sick of the great noise about *imprudences* and *disorders.* They have heard it so often from the mouths of opposers that they are prejudiced against the sound; and they are therefore rather confirmed in any practice, than brought off, by the clamor they hear against it. And to tell the truth, the cry of irregularity has been more in the mouths of enemies than others. This has so prejudiced the minds of some that they have been ready to think that all that has been said about errors and imprudences was from an ill spirit; and has confirmed them that there is no such thing as any prevailing imprudences. Herein the devil has had an advantage put into his hands.

If we look back into the history of the church, we may observe that it has been a common device of the devil, when he finds he can keep men quiet and secure no

longer to drive a revival of religion to excesses and extra-
vagances. He holds them back as long as he can, but when
he can do it no longer he will push them on and, if possible,
run them upon their heads. Yea, the principal means by
which the devil was successful, by degrees, to overset that
grand religious revival that was in the primitive ages of
Christianity was to improve the indiscreet zeal of Christians to drive them into those three extremes of
enthusiasm, superstition, and *severity towards opposers.*
This should be enough for an everlasting warning to the
Christian church.

It is a mistake I have observed in some, to their wound-
ing, that they think they are in no danger of going astray
because they are near to God. For persons in such a confidence to neglect watchfulness and care is a presumption
by which I have known many wofully ensnared. That
direction of Christ is never out of date in this world:
"Watch and pray always, that ye may be counted worthy
to escape all these things, and to stand before the Son of
man," (Luke 21:36). Though God stands ready to pro-
tect his people, especially those that are near to him, yet
he expects great care and labor of all; and whatever
spiritual privileges we are raised to, we have no warrant
to expect protection in any other way. It is therefore a
great error and sin in some persons that they are fixed in
their way in some things that others account errors, and
will not hearken to admonition and counsel, but are confident that they are in the right of it because they have
great degrees of the Spirit of God, (I Cor. 14:37-38).

First: In speaking of errors that have been, or that we
are in danger of, I would in the *first* place take notice of
the causes whence the errors that attend a great revival

of religion usually arise; and as I go along, take notice of some particular errors that arise from each of those causes.

(1) *Spiritual pride.* This is the main door by which the devil comes into the hearts of those that are zealous for the advancement of religion. It is by this that the mind defends itself in errors, and guards itself against light by which it might be corrected and reclaimed. It is most like the sin that the devil committed in a heaven of light and glory. It is the most hidden and difficultly discovered. Of all kinds of pride, spiritual pride is upon many accounts the most hateful. For this reason, the pride of those that are spiritually proud consists much in an high conceit of two things, viz. their *light* and their *humility;* both which are a strong prejudice against a discovery of pride, Psa. 19:12.

Spiritual pride is the most secret of all sins. It is a sin that has, as it were, many lives. If you kill it, it will live still; if you mortify and suppress it in one shape, it rises in another; if you think it is all gone, yet it is there still. There are a great many kinds of it that lie in different forms and shapes, one under another, and encompass the heart like the coats of an onion; if you pull off one there is another underneath. He that trusts his own heart is a fool.

It is true that great degrees of the spiritual presence of God tend greatly to mortify pride and all corruption; but yet, though in the experience of such favors there be much to restrain pride one way, there is much to tempt and provoke it another; and we shall be in great danger thereby without great watchfulness and prayerfulness. Let no saint, however eminent, think himself out of danger of this. The apostle Paul, doubtless as eminent a saint as any, was not out of danger even after he was admitted to God in the third heavens, by information he himself gives us, II Cor. 12.

Spiritual pride is very apt to suspect others. It has been the manner in some places, or at least the manner of some persons, to speak of almost everything that they see amiss in others in the most harsh, severe, and terrible language. What a strange device of the devil is here to overthrow all Christian meekness and gentleness, and to defile the mouths of the children of God. And it is a remarkable instance of the weakness of the human mind, and how much too cunning the devil is for us! How far shall we banish the appearance of humility, mutual honor, complacence, and an esteem of others above themselves, which ought to clothe the children of God?

Spiritual pride often disposes persons to singularity in external appearance, to affect a singular way of speaking, to use a different sort of dialect from others, or to be singular in voice or behavior. It disposes persons to affect separation, to stand at a distance from others as better than they. Its effect is a certain unsuitable and selfconfident boldness before God and men. There ought to be the utmost watchfulness against all such appearances of spiritual pride, in all that profess to have been the subjects of this work, and especially in the promoters of it.

The eminently humble Christian is as it were clothed with lowliness, meekness, and gentleness of spirit and behavior. Pure Christian humility disposes persons to honor all men, agreeable to I Pet. 2:17. It has no such thing as roughness, or contempt, or fierceness, or bitterness in its nature. I Pet. 5:5, Col. 3:12, Eph. 4:31. With such a spirit as this ought especially zealous ministers of the gospel to be clothed, and those that God is pleased to improve as instruments in his hands of promoting his work, II Tim. 2:24-25.

(2) *Wrong principles* from whence errors in conduct arise, that attend such a revival of religion.

(a) One erroneous principle which has proved mischievous to the present glorious work of God is a notion that it is God's manner to guide his saints, at least some that are more eminent, by inspiration or immediate revelation, and to make known to them what shall come to pass hereafter, or what it is his will that they should do, by impressions that he by his Spirit makes upon their mind, either with, or without, texts of Scripture; whereby something is made known to them that is not taught in the Scripture as the words lie in the Bible. Late experience, in some instances, has shown that the tendency of this notion is to cause persons to esteem the Bible as a book that is in a great measure useless.

This error will defend and support all errors. As long as a person has a notion that he is guided by immediate direction from Heaven, it makes him incorrigible and impregnable in all his misconduct. It is strange what a disposition there is in many well-disposed and religious persons to fall in with this. Some that follow impulses and impressions go away with a notion that they do no other than follow the guidance of God's Word because the impression is made with a text of Scripture, though they take that text and improve it as a new revelation, while the text in itself implies no such thing. This is quite a different thing from the Spirit's enlightening the mind to understand the precepts of the Word of God and know what is revealed in them, Rom. 12:2, I Cor. 12:31 - 13:1.

(b) Another way that many have been deceived is by drawing false conclusions from true premises. Many true saints have been led into arguing that they have prayed in faith; and that oftentimes, when the premises are true, they have been greatly assisted in prayer for a particular mercy and have had the true spirit of prayer in exercise in their asking it of God; but they have concluded more from these premises than is a just consequence from them. Their prayer is accepted and heard, and God will give a gracious answer, according to his own wisdom; this is a just consequence from it. But that God will answer them in that individual thing that they ask, if it be not a thing promised in God's word, or that will be for the good of God's church and the advancement of Christ's kingdom, is more than can be justly concluded from it. The ground on which some expect that they shall receive the thing they have asked for is rather a strong imagination than any true humble faith in the divine sufficiency. And sometimes the confidence that persons have that their prayers shall be answered is only a self-righteous confidence, and no true faith. Nothing is of greater importance than the degree of humility, poverty of spirit, self-emptiness and resignation to the holy will of God which God gives us the exercise of in our seeking that mercy.

(c) Another erroneous principle that has been a source of many errors in conduct is that persons ought always to do whatsoever the Spirit of God (though but indirectly) inclines them to. Indeed all that the Spirit of God inclines us to directly and immediately, without the intervention of any other cause that shall pervert, ought to be done. But there may be many things that we may be disposed to do, which disposition may indirectly be from the Spirit of God, that we ought not to do. For instance, the Spirit of God may cause a person to have a dear love to another, and delight in his comfort, ease and pleasure. This disposition in general is good; but yet, through indiscretion, he may kill him with kindness. The apostle does evidently suppose that the Spirit of God in his extraordinary influences on men's minds may, in some respect, excite inclinations in men that, if gratified, would tend to confusion, and therefore must sometimes be restrained, I Cor. 14:31-33.

(d) Another wrong principle is that whatsoever is found to be of present benefit may and ought to be practiced, without looking forward to future consequences. Some persons seem to think what is found to be for their present edification sufficiently justifies anything. Indeed, things being required by moral rules, or absolute positive commands of God, must be done, and future consequences left with God: but in other things we are to be governed by discretion, and we must look at the consequence. It is the duty of ministers especially to exercise this descretion. This is implied in those words of Christ to his disciples, when he sent them forth, Matt. 10:16: "Be ye wise as serpents." And the apostle Paul who, though he would not depart from his enjoined duty to please carnal men, yet wherein he could with a good conscience, did lay out himself to please them, and if possible to avoid raising in the multitude prejudices, oppositions, and tumults against the gospel; and looked upon it that it was of great consequence that it should be, if possible, avoided (I Cor. 10:32-33, 11:19:23, Rom. 15:1-2, 12:18, II Tim. 2:24-26, Rom. 14:16). So that the great and most zealous and most successful propagator of vital religion that ever was, looked upon it to be of great consequence to endeavor to avoid raising the prejudice and opposition of the world against religion.

I believe that saying of our Saviour, "I came not to send peace on earth, but division," has been abused, as though when we see strife and division about religion, it was to be rejoiced in. It has almost been laid down as a maxim by some that the more division and strife, the better sign;

which naturally leads persons to seek it and provoke it. Persons that are influenced by an indiscreet zeal are always too much in haste; they are impatient of delays, and therefore are jumping to the uppermost step first, before they have taken the preceding steps. It is a vain prejudice that some have lately imbibed against rules of prudence and moderation. They overshoot their mark, and frustrate their own end.

(e) Another error that some have gone upon is a wrong notion that they have of an attestation of divine providence to persons or things. We go too far when we look upon the success that God gives to some persons, in making them instruments of good, as a testimony of God's approbation of those persons. It is a main argument, made use of to defend the conduct of some ministers that have been blamed as imprudent and irregular, that God has smiled upon them and blessed them; and that however men charge them, yet it is evident that God is with them.

But persons may be misled. If a person's success be a reward of something that God sees in him, yet it is no argument that he approves of everything in him. Some, by the great success that God has given them, have been bold therefore to go to great lengths in a presumption that God was with them, and would defend them, and finally baffle all that found fault with them. We cannot safely take the events of providence as a revelation of God's mind concerning a person's conduct and behavior. God sometimes gave primitive Christians the influence of his Spirit when they were out of the way of duty; and continued it while they were abusing it, I Cor. 14:31-33.

(f) Another erroneous principle is that external order in religion, and use of the means of grace, is little to be regarded. It is spoken of lightly under the names of ceremonies and dead forms. It is objected that God does not

look at the outward form; he looks at the heart. That is a
weak argument. Zeal without order will do but little, or
at least it will be effectual but a little while, I Cor. 12:
14-31, Rom. 12:4-8. Order is one of the most necessary
means of the spiritual good of God's church.

It has been thought by some that there is no need that
such and such religious services and performances should
be limited to any certain office in the church. And also
that those offices, particularly the gospel ministry, need
not be limited to persons of a liberal education. Some
have been for having others of eminent experience publicly
licensed to preach, yea, and ordained to the work of the
ministry; and some ministers have favored such a thing.
But how little do they consider the unavoidable consequences of opening such a door? How shall we know
where to stop? If one is admitted because his experiences
are remarkable, another will think his experiences also
remarkable. Not but that there may be some persons in
the land, that have no education at college, that are in
themselves better qualified for the work of the ministry than
others that have taken degrees, and are now ordained. But
I believe the breaking over those bounds that have been
set would in its consequences be a greater calamity than
missing such persons in the work of the ministry.

(3) *Being ignorant* or unobservant of some particular
things by which the devil has special advantage.

(a) I would particularly take notice of some things
with respect to the inward experiences of Christians themselves. Oftentimes there is a mixture of that which is
natural with that which is divine. And indeed it is not to
be supposed that Christians ever have any experiences in
this world that are wholly pure, entirely spiritual, without
any mixture of what is natural and carnal. The seed, as
sent from heaven and planted in the heart, is pure, but as

it springs up out of the heart is impure. There is very often with that which is spiritual a great mixture of that affection or passion which arises from natural principles; often impressions on the imagination. There is a greater mixture of these things in the experiences of some Christians than other. We ought to be well aware of these that we may not take all for gold that glistens.

The unheeded defects there sometimes are in the experiences of true Christians, in the best of saints, are very much out of due proportion. The essence of truly Christian experiences is not wanting; but yet that is wanting that is needful to the proper beauty of the image of Christ in such a person's experiences. It is chiefly from such a defect that some things have arisen that have been pretty common among true Christians of late, that have been supposed by many to have risen from a good cause; but the proper cause has been sin, even that odious defect in their experience. The same is true in many cases of persons' unsuitable boldness, their disposition to speak with authority, intemperate zeal, and many other things that sometimes appear in true Christians, under great religious affections.

Another thing of which we should be aware is the degenerating of experiences. What I mean is something diverse from the mere decay of experiences, or their gradually vanishing. It is persons' experiences growing by degrees worse and worse in their kind, more and more partial and deficient; the spiritual part decreases, and the other useless and hurtful parts greatly increase. There is such a thing, and it is frequent.

Pride, above all things, promotes this degeneracy of experiences, because it grieves and quenches the Spirit of the Lamb of God, and so kills the spiritual part. The unhappy person, for the most part, is not sensible of his own calamity; but because he finds himself still violently

moved, and with greater heats of zeal, thinks himself fuller
of the Spirit of God than ever. It is with him as the apostle
says of the Galatians (Gal. 3:3): "Having begun in the
Spirit, they are made perfect by the flesh."

(b) Now to take notice of the external effects of
experiences which also give Satan an advantage. What I
have respect to is the secret and unaccountable influence
that custom has upon persons. By custom I mean both a
person's being accustomed to a thing in himself, in his
own common, allowed and indulged practice, and also
the countenance and approbation of others amongst whom
he dwells, by their general voice and practice. I am far
from ascribing all the late uncommon effects and outward manifestations of inward experiences to custom and
fashion, as some do. It would be unreasonable, and
prejudicial to the interest of religion to frown upon all
these manifestations of great religious affections. Yet I
think they greatly err who think that these things should
be wholly unlimited. Otherwise extraordinary outward
effects and show will increase, without any increase
of internal cause.

Second: I have taken notice of the more general causes
whence the errors that have attended this revival have
risen. I now proceed to take notice of some particular
errors that have risen from these causes. In some perhaps
they have been chiefly owing to one, and in others to another, and in others to the influence of several or all
conjunctly.

(1) *Censuring others* that are professing Christians,
in good standing in the visible church, as unconverted.
This is the worst disease that has attended this work, against
the plain and strict prohibitions of the Word of God, most
contrary to the spirit and rules of Christianity. The
manner of many has been, when they first enter into

conversation with any person that seems to make any pretense to religion, to fix a judgment of him from his manner of talking, whether he be converted or experimentally acquainted with vital piety or not; and then to treat him accordingly, and freely to express their thoughts of him to others, especially those that they have a good opinion of as true Christians. If they do not declare their minds expressly, yet by their manner of speaking of them, as least to their friends, they will show plainly what their thoughts are. So when they have heard any minister pray or preach, their first work has been to observe him on a design of discerning him, whether he be a converted man or not; whether he prays like one that feels the saving power of God's Spirit in his heart.

There has been an unhappy disposition in some ministers towards their brethren in the ministry in this respect, which has encouraged and greatly promoted such a spirit among some of their people. Nothing has been gained by this practice. Possibly some have openly censured ministers in hopes that the uneasiness would be so great that unconverted ministers would be cast off, and that then things would go on happily. But there is no likelihood of it. It is no hell peopling charity,* as some seem to suppose, that we do not treat them as Christians, because we have taken it upon us to pass judgment on their state. We should leave that work to Christ, who is the searcher of hearts, and to whom vengeance belongs; and not, without warrant, take the scourge out of his hand into our own. I have seen that which abundantly convinces me that the business is too high for me, Rom. 14:4, James 4:12.

As this practice ought to be avoided, so should all such open, visible marks of distinction that imply it; as par-

---

*This is Edwards' exact phrase.

ticularly, distinguishing such as we have judged to be in a converted state with the compellations of *brother* or *sister*. And some have a way of joining a sort of imprecations with their petitions for others that appear to me wholly needless and improper: they pray that others may either be converted or removed. I have never heard nor read of any such thing practiced in the church of God until now. If we give way to such things as these, where shall we stop?

(2) *Lay exhorting* is another thing I would take notice of, in the management of which there has been much error and misconduct. All exhorting one another of laymen is not unlawful or improper, but on the contrary, some exhorting is a Christian duty. But the great difficulty is to settle the bounds, and to tell exactly, how far laymen may go, and when they exceed their limits, which is a matter of so much difficulty that I do not wonder if many in their zeal have transgressed.

The common people, in exhorting one another, ought not to clothe themselves with the like authority with that which is proper for ministers. There is a certain authority that ministers have, and should exercise, in teaching, Rom. 10:15, Mal. 2:7, II Cor. 5:18-20, Tit. 2:15. But there is a great deal of difference between teaching as a father amongst a company of children, and counselling in a *brotherly* way. Those that are mere brethren ought not to assume authority in exhorting, though one may be better and have more experience than another. When private Christians admonish one another, it ought to be in a humble manner, rather by way of entreaty than with authority.

Thus I have taken particular notice of many of those things that have appeared to me amiss in the management of our religious concerns, relating to the present revival of religion: and have taken liberty freely to express my thoughts upon them. Upon the whole it appears manifest to me that things have as yet never been set a going in their right channel. If they had, and means had been blessed in proportion as they have been now, this work would have prevailed as before this time to have carried all before it, and have triumphed over New England as its conquest.

PART V

Shewing positively what ought to be done to promote this Work.

First: We ought to remove the stumbling blocks. "Cast ye up, cast ye up; prepare the way; take up the stumbling block out of the way of my people" (Isa. 57:14).

In order to do this there must be a great deal done at confessing faults, on both sides. There is hardly any duty more contrary to our disposition, and mortifying to pride, but it must be done. I am persuaded that those that have openly opposed this work, or have spoken lightly of it, cannot be excused in the sight of God without openly confessing their fault; especially if they be ministers. On the other side, if those that have been zealous to promote this work have done that which is contrary to Christian rules, whereby they have injured others, or greatly violated good order and so done that which has wounded religion, they must publicly confess it. For us to be judging one another, and behaving with fierceness and bitterness towards one another, is exceeding unsuitable, Psa. 37:11, 76:9, Isa. 29:19.

As such a time as this does require the exercise of a great deal of forbearance one towards another, so there is requisite the exercise of great patience in waiting on God. The beginning of a revival of religion will naturally and necessarily be attended with many difficulties. We cannot expect that, after a time of degeneracy and depravity in the church, things should all come to rights at once. Though the difficulty may be very great, God's people should wait patiently upon him. If they do so, they may expect that in his time he will appear for their deliverance.

Second: There are things that must be done, more directly to advance the work.

(1) It concerns every one to look into his own heart and see to it that he be a partaker of the benefits of the work himself. Though I judge not those that have opposed this work, and would not have others judge them, yet I would entreat them to leave off concerning themselves so much about others, and look into their own souls, and see to it that they are the subjects of a true, saving work of the Spirit of God.

The work has been chiefly amongst those that are young; comparatively few others have been made partakers of it. Indeed, it has commonly been so when God has begun any great revival. He has taken the young people, and has cast off the old and stiff-necked generation. Of the children of Israel in the wilderness, the younger generation seems to have been the most excellent generation that ever was in the church of Israel. Let the old generation in this land take heed that they do not refuse to be convinced by all God's wonders, and that they do not continue forever objecting; least, while God is bringing their children into a land flowing with milk and honey.

(2) It concerns us that are ministers to see to it that we are partakers of this work. We need a double portion of the Spirit of God at such a time as this, and we ought to give ourselves no rest until we have obtained it. And in order to this I think ministers, above all persons, ought to be much in prayer and fasting.

Two things that are needful in ministers, as they would advance the kingdom of Christ, are zeal and resolution. A man of ordinary capacity will do more with them, than one of ten times the parts and learning without them. Those that are possessed of these qualities commonly carry the day in almost all affairs. But while we are cold and heartless, and only go on in a dull manner, in an old formal round, we shall never do any great matters. We have many ministers that do not want for abilities; they are persons of bright parts and learning. They should consider how much they might do for Christ if they had in their hearts a heavenly warmth proportionable to their light.

With respect to candidates for the ministry, I will not undertake particularly to determine what kind of examination they should pass under, in order to their admission to that sacred work. Yet I will take the liberty to give my opinion with respect to those persons fit for the work of the ministry. Extraordinary means should be used for training up the students in vital religion, and experimental and practical godliness. There is a great deal of pains taken to teach scholars human learning; there ought to be as much, and more, care thoroughly to educate them in religion and lead them to true and eminent holiness.

(3) Rich men have a talent in their hands, in the disposal of which they might very much promote such a work as this. What a thousand pities it is that, for want of a heart, they commonly have no share at all. It seems to me that, in this age, most of us have but very narrow, penurious notions of Christianity, as it respects our use and disposal of temporal goods. The primitive Christians had not such notions. Great things might be done for the advancement of the kingdom of Christ, at this day, by those that have ability.

(4) The circumstances of the present work do loudly call God's people to abound in *fasting* and *prayer*. It is God's will that the prayers of his saints should be one great and principal means of carrying on the designs of Christ's kingdom in the world. I am sensible that considerable has been done in duties of this nature in some places; but I do not think so much as God, in the present dispensation of his providence, calls for (Isa. 62:6-7, Luke 18:7, Acts 1:13-14). There is no way that Christians in a private capacity can do so much to promote the work of God, and advance the kingdom of Christ, as by prayer. God is, if I may so say, at the command of the prayer of faith.

(5) It is incumbent upon God's people to take heed that, while they abound in external duties of devotion, such as praying, hearing, singing, and attending religious meetings, there be a proportionable care to abound in *moral duties,* such as acts of righteousness, truth, meekness, forgiveness and love towards our neighbor, which are of much greater importance in the sight of God than all the externals of his worship (Matt. 9:13, 12:7). The internal acts and principles of the worship of God are the most essential and important of all duties of religion, for therein consists the essence of all religion.

Of this inward religion, there are two sorts of external expressions. The one sort are outward acts of worship, such as meeting in religious assemblies, attending sacraments, and other outward institutions. The other sort are the expressions of our love to God, by obeying his moral commands, of self-denial, righteousness, meekness, and Christian love in our behavior among men. And the latter are of vastly the greatest importance in the Christian life. They are abundantly more insisted on by the prophets in the Old Testament, and Christ and his apostles in the

New. When these two kinds of duties are spoken of together, the latter are ever more greatly preferred (Isa. 1:12-18; 58:1-7; Micah 6:7-8; Zech. 7:1-10; Matt. 15:3; 23:14, 25, 34; James 2:8-26; I John 2:3, 7-11; Matt., chapter 25). External acts of worship are of little use, but as signs of inward worship. The external acts of worship, consisting in bodily gestures, words and sounds, are the cheapest part of religion, and least contrary to our lusts.

SUMMARY

Thus I have finished what I proposed. I have taken the more pains in it because it appears to me that now God is giving us the most happy season to attempt a universal reformation, that ever was given in New England. And it is a thousand pities that we should fail of that which would be so glorious for want of being sensible to our opportunity, or being aware of those things that tend to hinder it, or our taking improper course to obtain it, or not being sensible in what way God expects we should seek it. If it should please God to bless any means for convincing the country of his hand in this work, and bringing them fully and freely to acknowledge his glorious power and grace in it, and engage with one heart and soul to endeavor to promote it, it would be a dispensation of divine providence that would have a most glorious aspect, happily signifying the approach of great and glorious things to the church of God, and justly causing us to hope that Christ would speedily come to set up his kingdom of light, holiness, peace and joy on earth, as is foretold in his word . . . . Amen: Even so come Lord Jesus!

A Treatise Concerning
Religious Affections

A Treatise Concerning Religious Affections:
in Three Parts

INTRODUCTION

What are the distinguishing marks of those that are in
favor with God, and entitled to his eternal rewards? What
is the nature of true religion? And wherein lie the distinguishing notes of that virtue and holiness that is ac-
ceptable in the sight of God? But though it be of such
importance, and though we have clear and abundant light
in the Word of God to direct us in this matter, yet there
is no one point wherein professing Christians do more
differ one from another. It would be endless to reckon up
the variety of opinions in this point that divide up the
Christian world.

The consideration of these things has long engaged
me to this matter, with the utmost diligence and care,
and exactness of search and inquiry. I am sensible it is
difficult to judge impartially of that which is the subject
of this discourse. Many will be hurt to find so much that
appertains to religious affection here condemned: and
perhaps indignation and contempt will be excited in others
by finding so much here justified and approved. It may
be, some will be ready to charge me with inconsistence with
myself. It is a hard thing to be a hearty zealous friend of
what has been good and glorious in the late extraordinary
appearances, and to rejoice in it; and at the same time to

see the evil and pernicious tendency of what has been bad, and earnestly to oppose that. There is indeed something very mysterious that so much good and so much bad should be mixed together in the church of God.

It greatly concerns us to use our utmost endeavors clearly to discern wherein true religion does consist. Till this be done, it may be expected that great revivings of religion will be but of short continuance. I hope in the mercy of a gracious God for the acceptance of the sincerity of my endeavors.

PART I

Concerning the Nature of the Affections, and their Importance in Religion

"Whom having not seen, ye love; in whom, though now ye see him not, yet believing, ye rejoice with joy unspeakable, and full of glory," I Peter 1:8.

In these words, the apostle represents the state of the minds of Christians under persecution. He has respect to these persecutions in the two preceding verses when he speaks of *the trial of their faith,* and of *their being in heaviness through manifold temptations.*

Such trials are of benefit to true religion. Hereby the truth of it is manifested, and the genuine beauty and amiableness remarkably appear. True virtue never appears so lovely, as when it is most oppressed; and the divine excellency of Christianity is never exhibited with advantage, as when under the greatest trials. Such trials also tend to refine it, and deliver it from mixtures of that which is false. As gold that is tried in the fire is purged and comes forth more solid and beautiful, so true faith, tried as gold is tried, becomes more precious.

There are two kinds of exercise of true religion in them, under their sufferings, that the apostle takes notice of in the text, wherein these benefits appeared. They *loved Jesus Christ*, for they saw him spiritually whom the world saw not. And *joy in Christ*: though their outward sufferings were grievous, yet their inward spiritual joys were greater than their sufferings. Hence the doctrine that I would raise from these words is this: True religion, in great part, consists in holy affections.

The apostle singles out the religious affections of *love* and *joy*. These are the exercises of religion wherein their religion did appear true and pure, and in its proper glory.

First: It may be inquired what the affections of the mind are. The affections are no other than the more vigorous and sensible exercises of the inclination and will of the soul. God has endued the soul with two faculties. One is that by which it is capable of perception and speculation, or by which it discerns, and views, and judges of things, which is called the understanding. The other faculty is that by which the soul does not merely perceive things, but is some way inclined with respect to the things it considers, either *to* them or *from* them. This faculty is sometimes called the *inclination*, and as it has respect to the actions that are determined by it, is called the *will;* and the mind, with regard to the exercises of this faculty, is often called the *heart*. More vigorous and sensible exercises of this faculty are called the *affections*. The will, and the affections of the soul, are not two faculties. What are commonly called affections are not essentially different from actings of the will, but only in the degree and manner of exercise.

Such seems to be our nature that there never is any lively exercise of the will or inclination of the soul without some effect upon the body. Yet it is not the body, but the mind only, that is the proper seat of the affections. The body of a man is no more capable of being really the subject of love or hatred, joy or sorrow, fear or hope, than the body of a tree; or than the same body of man is capable of thinking and understanding. As it is the soul only that thinks, so it is the soul only that loves or hates, rejoices or is grieved at what it thinks of.

Affections and passions are frequently spoken of as the same; yet there is a difference. Affection is used for all lively actings of the will; but passion for those that are more sudden, whose effects on the animal spirits are more violent, and the mind overpowered and less in its own command.

As all the exercises of the will are either in approving or liking, or disapproving and rejecting, so the affections are of two sorts. Of the former are love, desire, hope, joy, gratitude, complacence; of the latter, hatred, fear, anger, grief, and such like. In some there is a composition of each; as in the affection of *pity*, there is something of the former towards the person suffering, and something of the latter toward what he suffers.

Second: Some things render it evident that true religion in great part consists in the affections.

(1) That religion which God requires, and will accept, does not consist in weak, dull, and lifeless wouldings, raising us but a little above a state of indifference. God, in his Word, insists that we be good in earnest, "fervent in spirit," and our hearts vigorously engaged in religion, Rom. 12:11, Deut. 6:4-5, 10:12, 30:6. In nothing is vigor in the actings of our inclinations so requisite; and in nothing is lukewarmness so odious.

True religion is evermore a powerful thing; and the power of it appears first in the inward exercises of it, in the heart, where is the principal and original seat of it.

Hence true religion is called the *power of godliness*, in distinction from the external appearances of it, that are the *form* of it, II Tim. 1:7, 3:5, Luke 24:32.

(2) The Author of human nature has not only given affections to men, but has made them very much the spring of men's actions. As affections do not only necessarily belong to human nature, but are a very great part of it; so by regeneration holy affections do not only necessarily belong to true religion, but are a very great part of it. We see the world of mankind to be exceeding busy and active; and the affections of men are the springs of the motion. Take away all love and hatred, all hope and fear, all anger, zeal, and affectionate desire, and the world would be, in a great measure, motionless and dead. So in religious matters, the spring of actions is very much religious affection. He that has doctrinal knowledge and speculation only, without affection, never is engaged in the business of religion.

(3) The things of religion take hold of men's souls no further than they affect them. There are multitudes that often hear the Word of God, and all that is heard seems to make no alteration in their disposition or behavior. The reason is, they are not affected with what they hear. I am bold to assert that there never was any considerable change wrought in the mind or conversation of any person, by anything of a religious nature, that had not his affections moved. Nor was there ever a saint awakened out of a cold, lifeless frame, or recovered from a declining state in religion, without having his heart affected.

(4) The Holy Scriptures do everywhere place religion very much in the affections; such as fear, hope, love, hatred, desire, joy, sorrow, gratitude, compassion, and zeal. The texts in which this is manifest, both in the Old Testament and New, are innumerable.

True godliness is very commonly called by the name of *the fear of God.* Hope: I Cor. 13:13, Jer. 17:7, Psa. 31:24, 146:5, 33:18, 147:11, Rom. 8:24, I Thess. 5:8, Heb. 6:19, I Pet. 1:3. Hatred: Prov. 8:13, Psa. 97:10, 101:2-3, 119:104, 139:21. Holy desire: Isa. 26:8, Psa. 27:4, 42:1-2, 84:1-2, Matt. 5:6, Rev. 21:6. Holy joy: Psa. 37:4, 97:12, Matt. 5:12, Phil. 3:1, 4:4, I Thess. 5:16, Gal. 5:22. Religious sorrow, mourning, and brokenness of heart: Matt. 5:4, Psa. 34:18, Isa. 61:1-2, Psa. 51:17. And the exercise of true religion appears in *love,* and *gratitude,* in *compassion,* and *zeal.* I have mentioned but a few texts which place religion very much in the affections.

(5) The Scriptures represent true religion as summarily comprehended in love, the chief of the affections, and fountain of all other affections. So our blessed Saviour represents the matter, Matt. 22:37-40. And the apostle Paul does from time to time make the same representation (as in Rom. 13:8, Gal. 5:14, I Tim. 1:5), and speaks of love as the greatest thing in religion, the essence of it, and the fountain from whence proceeds all that is good, I Cor. 13.

Now, although it be true that the love thus spoken of includes the whole of a sincerely benevolent propensity of the soul towards God and man, yet, when in sensible and vigorous exercise, it is no other than affectionate love. Surely it is such vigorous and fervent love which Christ speaks of, as the sum of all religion, when he speaks of loving God with all our hearts, with all our souls, and with all our minds. The essence of all true religion lies in holy love. And in like manner, from a fervent love to men will arise all other virtuous affections toward men.

(6) The religion of the most eminent saints we have in the Scripture consisted much in holy affections. Notice

David, that "man after God's own heart," who has given
us a lively portraiture of his religion in the Psalms. Those
holy songs he has left us are nothing else but the expressions and breathings of devout and holy affections. Another is the apostle Paul. By what is said of him in the
Scripture, he appears to have been a person that was full
of affection. And it is very manifest that the religion he
expresses in his epistles consisted very much in holy affections. It appears that he was inflamed, actuated, and
entirely swallowed up by a most ardent love to his Lord,
II Cor. 5:14-15, II Thess. 2:7-8, II Cor. 2:4, 12:19,
II Tim. 1:2, Phil. 1:8, II Cor. 6:11. The same apostle
is often expressing the affection of *joy,* and *hope,* and
zeal. The cause of his Master was mighty in him, continually inflaming his heart. The other instance is the
apostle John. It is evident by all his writings that he
was a person remarkably full of affection, unless we should
transcribe all his writings.

(7) He whom God sent into the world to be the light
of the world, the head of the church, the perfect example
of true religion and virtue, even the Lord Jesus Christ
was a person who was remarkably of a tender and affectionate heart. He was the greatest instance of ardency, vigor
and strength of love, to both God and man, that ever was,
John 2:17, Mark 3:5, Luke 19:41-42, 22:15, Matt.
15:32, John, chapters 13, 14, 15, 16, 17.

(8) The religion of heaven consists very much in affection. According to the Scripture representation of the
heavenly state, religion consists chiefly in holy and mighty
love and joy, and the expression of these in most fervent
and exalted praises. There is a sensation of the mind which
loves and rejoices, that is antecedent to any effects on the
body. This sensation of the mind does not depend on these
motions in the body, and so may be in the soul without

the body. Hence, the religion of heaven, consisting chiefly in holy love and joy, consists very much in affection; and therefore, undoubtedly, true religion consists very much in affection.

(9) This appears from the nature and design of the ordinances and duties which God hath appointed, as means and expressions of true religion.

(10) It is an evidence that true religion lies very much in affection of the heart, that the Scriptures place the sin of the heart in hardness of heart, Mark 3:5; Rom. 2:5; Ezek. 3:7; Heb. 3:8, 12, 13.

Third: Having considered the evidence of the proposition, I proceed to some inferences.

(1) Because many who, in the late extraordinary season, appeared to have great religious affections, seem to be so soon come to nothing, hence religious affections in general are grown out of credit with great numbers, as though religion did not at all consist in them. Thus we run from one extreme to another. Three or four years ago there was a prevalent disposition to look upon all high religious affections as eminent exercises of true grace. But of late, it is a thing much more prevalent to reject and discard all without distinction. Herein appears the subtilty of Satan. For although to true religion there must indeed be something else besides affection; yet true religion consists so much in the affections, that there can be no true religion without them. As on the one hand, where there is heat without light there can be nothing divine or heavenly in the heart, so on the other hand, where there is a kind of light without heat, a head stored with speculations, there can be nothing divine in that light. There are false affections, and there are true. A man's having much affection does not prove that he has

any true religion. But if he has no affection, it proves that he has no true religion.

(2) If true religion lies much in the affections, we may infer that such means are to be desired as have a tendency to move the affections. Such books, such a way of preaching the Word, and administration of ordinances, and such a way of worshipping God in prayer, and singing praises, is much to be desired.

(3) If true religion lies much in the affections, we have to be ashamed before God that we are no more affected with the great things of religion. How common is it among mankind that their affections are much exercised and engaged in other matters than in religion! In things which concern men's worldly interest, their hearts are tender and sensible, easily moved, deeply impressed. But how insensible and unmoved are most men about the great things of another world. How great cause have we to be humbled to the dust that we are no more affected.

PART II

Shewing what are no certain signs that Religious Affections are truly gracious, or that they are not.

As we have observed, we ought not to reject and condemn as though true religion did not at all consist in affection. So, on the other hand, we ought not to approve of all, as though every one that was religiously affected had true grace.

I would mention some things which are no signs one way or the other.

(1) It is no sign one way or the other that religious affections are very great, or raised very high. Love is an affection, but will any Christian say men ought not to love God and Jesus Christ in a high degree? And will any say

we ought not to have a very great hatred of sin, and a very deep sorrow for it? The Scriptures often require us to exercise very high affections. "Thou shalt love the Lord thy God with all thy heart, with all thy soul, with all thy mind, and with all thy strength." Also Psa. 119:97, 136; John 3:29-30; Matt. 28:8; and others. They greatly err who condemn persons as enthusiasts, merely because their affections are very high.

On the other hand, it is no evidence that religious affections are of a spiritual and gracious nature because they are great. Paul speaks of affections which had been exceedingly elevated, and he yet manifestly speaks as fearing that they were vain and had come to nothing, Gal. 4:15. So great multitudes made a mighty ado when Jesus entered into Jerusalem, as though the ground were not good enough for the ass he rode to tread upon. And how quickly was this ado at an end?

(2) It is no sign that affections have the nature of true religion, or that they have not, that they have great effects on the body. As was observed before, such is our nature, and such are the laws of union of soul and body, that the mind can have no lively or vigorous exercise without some effect upon the body. But great effects on the body certainly are no sure evidence that affections are spiritual. Nor, on the other hand, do I know any rule to determine that gracious and holy affections cannot have a great effect on the body. No such rule can be drawn from reason, and no such rule has yet been produced from the Scripture.

(3) It is no sign that affections are truly gracious, or that they are not, that they cause those who have them to be fluent, fervent, and abundant in talking of the things of religion. There are many persons who, if they see this in others, are greatly prejudiced against them. On the other

hand, there are many who, if they see this effect, are forward to determine that they are true children of God. That persons are disposed to be abundant in talking of things of religion may be from a good cause, and it may be from a bad one. "Out of the abundance of the heart the mouth speaketh."

(4) It is no sign that affections are gracious, or that they are otherwise, that persons did not excite them of their own contrivance, and by their own strength. Some declare that what they are conscious of seems to them evidently not to be from themselves, but from the mighty power of the Spirit of God; and others from hence condemn them, and determine what they experience is not from the Spirit of God, but from themselves, or from the devil. We are directed not to believe every spirit, but to try the spirits, whether they be of God.

(5) It is no sign that religious affections are truly holy and spiritual, or that they are not, that they come with texts of Scripture, remarkably brought to mind. All that can be argued from the purity and perfection of the Word of God, with respect to experiences, is this, that those experiences which are agreeable to the Word of God are right and cannot be otherwise; and not that those affections must be right which arise on occasion of the Word of God coming to the mind. What evidence is there that the devil cannot bring texts of Scripture to the mind, and misapply them to deceive persons, Matt. 4:1-11, II Pet. 3:16?

(6) There may be a great variety of false affections together that may resemble gracious affections. It is evident that there are counterfeits of all kinds. Persons may seem to have love to God and Christ, yet have no grace, Matt. 24:12-13. As from true divine love flow all Christian affections, so from counterfeit love flow other false

affections. So a resemblance of godly sorrow from sin, as in Pharaoh, Saul, and Ahab. So of spiritual joy, as in the stony-ground hearers, Matt. 13:20-21. So graceless persons may have earnest religious desires, which may be like Balaam's desires, Numb. 23:9-10. There is sometimes a very great similitude between true and false experiences, in their appearance, and in what is expressed and related by the subjects of them.

(7) Nothing can certainly be determined concerning the nature of the affections, by this, that comforts and joys seem to follow awakenings and convictions of conscience, in a certain order. Many persons seem to be prejudiced against affections that come in such a method as has been insisted on by many divines; first, awakenings, fears, and awful apprehensions; followed with legal humblings, in a sense of total sinfulness and helplessness, and then such and such light and comfort. But such prejudices and objections are without reason or Scripture. Surely it cannot be unreasonable to suppose that, before God delivers persons from a state of sin, they may understand their own salvation, and know something of what God does for them. If we consider extraordinary manifestations to saints of old, we shall find that God commonly first manifested himself in a way which was terrible, and then by those things that were comfortable. So it was with Moses at Mount Sinai, with Elijah (I Kings 19), with Daniel (Dan. 10), with the apostle John (Rev. 1). Christians are spoken of as those "that have fled for refuge, to lay hold on the hope set before them," Heb. 6:18. And it seems to be the natural import of the *gospel*, glad tidings, that it is news of deliverance and salvation after great fear and distress. From these things it appears unreasonable in professing Christians to make this an objection against the truth and spiritual nature of the com-

fortable and joyful affections which any have, that they follow such awful apprehensions and distresses.

On the other hand, it is not evidence that comforts and joys are right because they succeed great terrors and amazing fears of hell. Though convictions of conscience often cause terror, yet they do not consist in it, and terrors often arise from other causes. The terrors which some persons have are very much owing to the particular constitution and temper they are of. Some persons' imaginations are more strongly impressed with everything they are affected with than others. The impression on the imagination reacts on the affection, and raises that still higher; and so affection and imagination act reciprocally, till the person loses all possession of himself. And some speak of a great sight they have of their wickedness who, really, when the matter comes to be examined, have little or no convictions of conscience. There is no certain sign that the light and comforts which follow are true and saving. And for these following reasons:

(a) As the devil can counterfeit all the saving operations and graces of the Spirit of God, so he can counterfeit those operations that are preparatory to grace.

(b) If the operations and effects of the Spirit of God in convictions and comforts of true converts may be sophisticated, then the order of them may be imitated.

(c) We have no certain rule to determine how far God's own Spirit may go in those operations and convictions which in themselves are not spiritual and saving, and yet the person that is the subject of them never be converted, but fall short of salvation at last.

(d) Experience does greatly confirm that persons seeming to have convictions and comforts following one another in such a method and order, as is frequently observable in true converts, is no certain sign of grace.

(8) It is no certain sign that religious affections have in them the nature of true religion, or that they have not, that they dispose persons to spend much time in religion, and to be zealously engaged in external duties of worship. It is plain from the Scripture that it is the tendency of true grace to cause persons to delight in such religious exercises (Luke 2:37, Acts 2:46-47, Psa. 55:17). On the other hand, such a disposition is found in many that have no grace. So it was with the Pharisees; they "made long prayers, and fasted twice a week." False religion may cause persons to be loud and earnest in prayer (Isa. 58:4).

(9) It is no sign that affections are right, or that they are wrong, that they make persons exceeding confident that what they experience is divine, and that they are in good estate. It is an argument with some that there is no such thing to be expected in the church of God as a full and absolute assurance of hope; unless it be in some very extraordinary circumstances. It is manifest that it was a common thing for the saints we have a history of Scripture, to be assured. God, in the plainest manner revealed his favor to Noah, Abraham, Isaac, Jacob, Moses, Daniel, and others. Job says, "I know that my redeemer liveth." David almost everywhere speaks without hesistancy of God as his God. Christ was not afraid of speaking positively and plainly. It is evident that it is agreeable with his designs that there should be sufficient and abundant provision made, that his saints might have full assurance of their future glory. The apostle Paul, through all his epistles, speaks in an assured strain. And God's declared design in all this is that the heirs of the promises might have an undoubting hope, in an assurance of their future glory, Heb. 6:17-18. It further appears that assurance is not only attainable in some very extraordinary cases, but that

all Christians are directed to give all diligence to make their calling and election sure, II Pet. 1:5-8.

On the other hand, it is no sufficient reason to determine that men are saints because they are attended with an exceeding confidence that their state is good, and their affections divine. An overbearing, high-handed sort of confidence has not the countenance of a true Christian assurance. It savors more of the spirit of the Pharisees, who never doubted but that they were saints, and were bold to go to God, and thank him for the distinction he had made between them and other men. When once a hypocrite is thus established in a false hope, he has not those things to cause him to call his hope in question that oftentimes are the occasion of the doubting of true saints.

There are two sorts of hypocrites: one that are deceived with their outward morality and external religion, and the other are those who often cry down works, and men's own righteousness, and talk much of free grace; but at the same time make a righteousness of their humiliation, and exalt themselves to heaven with them. These two kinds of hypocrites, Mr. Shepard, in his exposition of the Parable of the Ten Virgins, distinguishes by the names of legal and evangelical hypocrites.

And here I cannot but observe that there are certain doctrines often preached to the people which need to be delivered with more caution and explanation than they frequently are. The doctrines I speak of are those of "Christians living by faith, not by sight; their giving glory to God, by trusting him in the dark; living upon Christ, and not upon experiences; not making their good frames the foundation of their faith." Which are excellent and important doctrines rightly understood, but corrupt and destructive as many understand them.

(10) Nothing can be certainly concluded concerning the nature of religious affections from this, that the outward manifestations of them are pleasing to the truly godly, and as such as gain their charity and win their hearts. The true saints have not such a spirit of discerning that they can certainly determine who are godly and who are not. For though they know experimentally what true religion is, in the internal exercises of it, yet these are what they can neither feel, nor see, in the heart of another. Wise and experienced men will proceed with great caution.

When there are many probable appearances of piety in others, it is the duty of the saints to receive them cordially into their charity, and to love them and rejoice in them, as their brethren in Christ Jesus. But yet the best of men may be deceived. It has been a common thing in the church of God for such bright professors, that are received as eminent saints among the saints, to fall away and come to nothing. This we need not wonder at. They may have religious affections of many kinds together, yet be without a spark of grace in their hearts. Counterfeit love and joy may be carried to a great height. How great may the resemblance be, as to all outward expressions, between a hypocrite and a saint!

Many suppose it to be real piety when others' talk seems to harmonize with their own experience. But there is not that certainty in such things which many imagine. If he uses the same words, which are commonly made use of, to express the affections of true saints, and also speaks boldly with an air of assurance, no wonder the other thinks his experiences harmonize with his own. So new converts may appear fair; and yet all may come to nothing.

It is with professors of religion, especially such as become so in a time of outpouring of the Spirit of God, as it is with blossoms in the spring; there are vast numbers of them upon the trees, which all look fair and promising; but yet many of them never come to anything. I know of no counsels which Christ ever delivered more plainly to guide us in our judging of others' sincerity, viz. that we should judge of the tree chiefly by the fruit. I believe many saints have gone much out of the way of Christ's words in this respect.

PART III

Shewing what are Distinguishing Signs of Truly Gracious and holy Affections

I come now to notice some things wherein those affections that are spiritual and gracious differ from those that are not so. But before I proceed directly to the distinguishing characters, I would previously mention some things concerning the marks I shall lay down.

(1) I am far from undertaking to give such signs of gracious affections as shall be sufficient to enable any certainly to distinguish true religion from false in others. In doing so I should be guilty of that arrogance I have been condemning.

(2) No signs are to be expected that shall be sufficient to enable saints certainly to discern their own good estate. Every saint living, whether strong or weak, and those who are in a bad frame, as well as others, cannot certainly know their good estate by them. It is not God's design that men should obtain assurance in any other way than by mortifying corruption, and increasing in grace, and obtaining the lively exercises of it. And although self-examination be a duty of great use and importance, and by no means to be neglected, yet it is not the principal means by which saints get satisfaction of their good estate. Assurance is not to be obtained so much by *self-examina-*

tion, as by *action.* The apostle Paul sought assurance chiefly this way, even by "forgetting the things that were behind, and reaching forth unto those things that were before." And it was by this means chiefly that he obtained assurance. "I therefore so run, not as uncertainly" (I Cor. 9:26). Therefore, though good rules to distinguish true grace from counterfeit may tend to convince hypocrites, and be of great use to the saints, yet I am far from pretending to lay down any such rules as shall be sufficient, without other means, to enable all true saints to see their good estate.

(3) There is not much encouragement to lay down rules or marks to distinguish between true and false affections, in hopes of convincing any considerable number of that sort of hypocrites who have been deceived with false affections, and are once settled in a false confidence and high conceit of their own supposed great experiences and privileges.

First: Affections that are truly spiritual and gracious arise from those influences and operations on the heart which are spiritual, supernatural, and divine. True saints, those who are sanctified by the Spirit of God, are in the New Testament called spiritual persons; and this is their peculiar character. Those who are spiritual are set in opposition to those who are natural and carnal (I Cor. 2:14-15). And as saints are called spiritual, so there are certain qualities and principles that have the same epithet given them (Rom. 8:6-7, Col. 1:9, Eph. 1:3).

Now it may be observed that the epithet *spiritual,* in these and other parallel texts of the N. T., is not used to signify any relation of persons or things to the spirit or soul of man, in opposition to the body which is the material part. Qualities are not said to be spiritual because they have their seat in the soul and not in the body. Nor

are things called spiritual because they are not corporeal.
But it is with relation to the Spirit of God that persons
or things are termed spiritual. Christians are called spiritual, and things are called spiritual, as related to the
Spirit of God (I Cor. 2:13, 14, Rom. 8:6). And it must
be observed that it was not by men's having the gifts of
the Spirit, but by their having the virtues of the Spirit
that they were called spiritual; as is apparent by Gal. 6:1
So that although natural men may be the subjects of many
influences of the Spirit of God (e.g. Num. 24:2, I Sam.
10:10, 16:14, I Cor. 13:1-3, Heb. 6:4-6) yet they are
not, in the sense of Scripture, spiritual persons.

(1) The Spirit of God is given to true saints to dwell
in them and to influence their hearts, as a principle of
new nature. The Scriptures represent the Holy Spirit as
dwelling in them as his temple, his proper abode and
everlasting dwelling place (I Cor. 3:16, II Cor. 6:16,
John 14:16-17). And he is represented as being there so
united to the faculties of the soul, that he becomes a
spring of new life.

(2) The Spirit of God so dwells in the hearts of the
saints that he there exerts and communicates himself in
his own proper nature. The grace that is begotten in the
hearts of the saints is something of the same nature with
that Spirit (John 3:6), and so is properly called a spiritual nature. Not that the saints are made partakers of
the essence of God, and so are *godded* with God, and
christed with Christ; but, to use the Scripture phrase, they
are made partakers of God's fulness (Eph. 3:17-19, John
1:16). From hence it follows that, in those gracious
exercises and affections which are wrought in the minds
of the saints through the saving influences of the Spirit of
God, there is a new inward perception or sensation of their
minds, entirely different in its nature and kind, and which

could be produced by no exalting, varying or compounding of perceptions or sensations which the mind had before. This new spiritual sense, and the new dispositions that attend it, are no new faculties, but are new principles of the nature. It is not a new faculty of understanding, but it is a new foundation laid in the nature of the soul.

From hence it appears that impressions which some have made on their imagination, or the imaginary ideas which they have of God, or Christ, or anything appertaining to religion, have nothing in them that is spiritual, or of the nature of true grace. Though such things may attend what is spiritual, and be mixed with it, yet in themselves they have nothing that is spiritual, nor are they any part of gracious experience. Some have had impressed upon them ideas of a great outward light, and this they call a spiritual discovery of Christ's glory. Some have had ideas of Christ's hanging on the cross, and his blood running from his wounds, and this they call a spiritual sight of Christ crucified, and the way of salvation by his blood. Some have seen him with his arms open ready to embrace them, and this they call a discovery of the sufficiency of Christ's grace and love, etc. The common, and less understanding, sort of people are the more easily led into apprehensions that these things are spiritual things; because, spiritual things being invisible, we are forced to use figurative expressions in speaking of them. But it is exceedingly apparent that such ideas have nothing in them which is spiritual or divine. There is nothing in their nature which requires that peculiar and unparalleled exercise of the power of God in order to their production.

(3) The immediate suggesting of the words of Scripture to the mind has nothing in it which is spiritual. It may be that persons have gracious affections going with the words of some great and high promises of Scripture which

come to their minds, and they look upon the words as directed immediately, spoken by God that moment, to them. These affections are built on no spiritual foundation. Balaam might know that the words which God suggested to him were indeed suggested by God, and yet have no spiritual knowledge.

What many persons call their conversion is after this manner. After awakening and terror, some comfortable promise comes suddenly to their minds, and the manner of its coming makes them conclude it comes from God. From hence they take their first encouragement to trust in Christ, because he has already revealed that he loves them, and has already promised eternal life. This is very absurd; it is God's manner to reveal his love and promises to men after they have believed, and not before. No promise of the covenant of grace belongs to any man until he has first believed in Christ, for it is by faith alone that we become interested in Christ, and the promises of the new covenant were made in him.

But here some may be ready to say, What, is there no such thing as any particular spiritual application of the promises of Scripture by the Spirit of God? I answer, There is doubtless such a thing as a spiritual and saving application of the invitations and promises of Scripture to the souls of men, but it is also certain that the nature of it is wholly misunderstood by many persons. The spiritual application of a Scripture promise does not consist in its being immediately suggested to the thoughts by some extrinsic agent. A spiritual application of the Word of God consists in applying it to the heart in spiritually enlightening, sanctifying influences.

(4) What many persons call the witness of the Spirit, that they are the children of God, has nothing in it spiritual or divine; and consequently the affections built

upon it are vain and delusive. That which many call the witness of the Spirit is no other than an immediate suggestion and impression that they are converted. This notion greatly debases that high operation of the Spirit which there is in the true witness of the Spirit. The word *witness* has misled many. The witness of the Spirit (Rom. 8:14-16) is elsewhere in the New Testament called the seal of the Spirit (II Cor. 1:22, Eph. 1:13-14). And the seal of the Spirit is a kind of effect on the heart which natural men are so far from being the subjects of, that they can have no manner of notion or idea of it. Many have been the mischiefs that have arisen from that false notion of the witness of the Spirit, that it is a kind of inward suggestion from God to man that he is beloved of him.

Second: The first objective ground of gracious affections is the transcendently excellent nature of divine things as they are themselves, and not any conceived relation they bear to self or self-interest.

It was before observed that love is the fountain of all affection, and particularly that Christian love is the fountain of all gracious affections. Now the glory of God and Jesus Christ is the primary reason why a true saint loves these things; not any benefit he has or shall receive from them, or any imagined relation which they bear to his interest, that self-love can properly be said to be the foundation of his love to these things.

Some say that all love arises from self-love; and that it is impossible for any man to love God, or any other being, but that love to himself must be the foundation of it. But I humbly suppose it is for want of consideration that they say so. A man must first love God before he will esteem God's good his own. There is a kind of affection that a man may have, a preconceived relation to himself, or some benefit already received, which does properly arise from self-love. That kind of affection to Jesus Christ cannot be truly gracious and spiritual: for self-love is a principle entirely natural (Luke 6:32, Job 1:9). They whose affection to God is founded on his profitableness to them begin at the wrong end.

There is a certain gratitude one has towards God, for loving him, or for something in him that suits self-love. It may arise from a false notion of God that men have been educated in; they love a God of their own imaginations. It may arise from an opinion of the favor of God to them, as the foundation of their love to him. Many have a false notion of communion with God, as though it were carried on by impulses, and whispers, and external representations immediately made to their imagination. As this sort of persons begin, so they go on. They have a conceit of God's love to them; acknowledgment of God's glory depends on regard to private interest. Self-love is not excluded from a gracious attitude (Psa. 116:1), but something else is included.

This is the main difference between the joy of the hypocrite and the joy of the true saint. The former rejoices in himself, the latter rejoices in God. The hypocrite talks more of the discovery than of the Christ discovered. The delight of a true saint is in God's perfection and Christ's beauty. Truly gracious affections have their foundation out of self, in God and Jesus Christ.

Third: The beginning of all truly holy affections is a love to divine things for their moral excellency. I will explain what I mean by moral excellency.

The word *moral* is not to be understood according to the common acceptation of the word, meaning an outward conformity to the duties of the moral law. It must be observed that divines make a distinction between moral good and evil, and natural good and evil. Moral good is that which is contrary to sin. Natural good is that which suits nature, without any relation to any rule of right and wrong. By moral evil they mean the evil of sin; by natural evil, that which is contrary to mere nature, without any respect to a rule of duty. Suffering is called natural evil, such as pain and torment, disgrace, natural defects, and the like. On the other hand, moral evil is that which is contary to right.

So divines make a distinction between the natural and moral perfections of God. By the moral perfections they mean those attributes which God exercises as a moral agent, such as his righteousness, truth, faithfulness and goodness, or, in a word, his holiness. By his natural attributes they mean those wherein consist his greatness, such as his power, knowledge, his being eternal, and his omnipresence.

Holiness comprehends all the true moral excellency of intelligent beings, and holiness in man is but the image of God's holiness. There is a twofold image of God in man; moral or spiritual, which is his holiness; natural, consisting in man's reason or understanding. That intelligent being, whose will is truly right and lovely, is morally good or excellent. Therefore his true love to God must begin with a delight in his holiness, and not with a delight in any other attribute. A holy love has a holy object. It consists in this, that it is the love of that which is holy for its holiness.

By this you may examine your love to God, and to Jesus Christ, and to the Word of God, and also your love to the people of God, and your desires after heaven, whether it be from a supreme delight in this sort of beauty, without being primarily moved from your imagined interest in them, or expectations from them. The grace of God may appear lovely two ways, either as *bonum utile,* a profitable good to me, which serves my interest and self-love, or as *bonum formosum,* a beautiful good in itself. The true saints have their hearts affected, and love captivated, by the free grace of God in the first place.

Fourth: Gracious affections arise from the mind's being enlightened spiritually to understand divine things; not heat without light, but from actual knowledge. The child of God is graciously affected because he understands something more of divine things than he did before (I John 4:7, Phil. 1:9, Rom. 10:2, Col. 3:10). Knowledge opens the hard heart and enlarges the affections (Luke 11:52).

Affections which do not arise from any light in the understanding are not spiritual, let them be ever so high. Persons suddenly excited of some shape or some shining light, become never the wiser by such things in the doctrine of the gospel. There is a distinction to be made between a mere notional understanding, wherein the mind only beholds things in the exercise of a speculative faculty, and the sense of the heart, wherein the mind does not only speculate and behold, but relishes and feels (Rom. 2:20). Spiritual understanding consists in "a sense of the heart, of the supreme beauty and sweetness of the holiness or moral perfection of divine things, together with all that discerning and knowledge of things of religion, that depends upon, and flows from such a sense."

The light which is given by the common influences of the Spirit of God consists only in a further understanding, through the assistance of natural principles, of those things which men may know, in some measure, by the alone ordinary exercise of their faculties. This consists only in the knowledge of those things pertaining to religion which are natural. Thus, for instance, in those convictions of conscience that natural men are often subject to, the Spirit of God assists the mind to a clearer idea of the natural perfections of God, wherein consists, not his beauty and glory, but his awful and terrible greatness. And in those common illuminations which are sometimes given to natural men, exciting in them some kind of religious desire, love, and joy, the mind is only assisted to a clearer apprehension of the natural good that is in divine things. There are many things exhibited in the gospel concerning God and Christ, and the way of salvation, that have a natural good in them, which suits the natural principle of self-love. All that love which natural men have to God is from no higher principle than their love of a man's good nature.

From what has been said, it appears that spiritual understanding does not consist in any new doctrinal knowledge, in opening to mind the mystical meaning of Scripture in its parables, types, and allegories. Many men can explain these who have no spiritual knowledge (I Cor. 13:2). It is also evident that it is not spiritual knowledge for persons to be informed of the will of God by immediate inward suggestions or by some text of Scripture suddenly brought to their minds. Spiritually to understand the Scripture is rightly to understand what is in the Scripture, and *what was in it before it was understood* (Luke 12:57, Rom. 12:2). In that leading of the Spirit, which is peculiar to God's children, is imparted that true wisdom, and holy discretion, so often spoken of in the Word of God, consisting most essentially in a divine supernatural sense and relish of the heart.

The *supposed* leading of the Spirit to do the will of God in outward behavior is either by exciting the idea of words (which are outward things) in their minds, either words of Scripture or other words, which they look upon as an immediate command of God, or else by exciting and impressing strongly the ideas of the outward actions themselves. Such sort of experiences raise the affections to a great height, and make a mighty uproar in both soul and body. In such things consisted the experiences of the Pythagoreans, who had strange ecstacies and raptures. And in such things seem to have consisted the experiences of the Essenes. And in such things consisted the pretended immediate converse with God and Christ and saints and angels of heaven, of the Monks, Anchorites, and Recluses that formerly abounded in the Church of Rome. In such things consisted the pretended experiences, and great spirituality, of many sects of enthusiasts that swarmed in the world after the Reformation. And in these things seems to lie the religion of the many kinds of enthusiasts of the present day. When the Spirit of God is poured out to begin a glorious work, then the old serpent, as fast as possible, introduces this bastard religion and mingles it with the true; which from time to time soon brings all things into confusion. Great and strict therefore should be the watch and guard that ministers maintain against such things, especially at a time of great awakening: for the common people are easily bewitched with such things. The imagination or phantasy seems to be that wherein are formed all those delusions of Satan. And this seems to be the reason why persons that are under the disease of melancholy are commonly so visibly and remarkably subject to the suggestions and temptations of Satan. The brain being thus weakened and diseased, it is less under the command of the higher faculties of the soul, and yields the more easily to extrinsic impressions.

I would say (to prevent misunderstanding of what has been said) that I am far from determining that no affections are spiritual which are attended with imaginary ideas. Such is the nature of man that he can scarcely think of anything intensely, without some kind of outward ideas, especially in persons of some constitutions of body. But there is a great difference between these two things, viz., lively imaginations arising from strong affections, and strong affections arising from lively imaginations.

Fifth: Truly gracious affections are attended with a reasonable and spiritual conviction of the judgment, of the reality and certainty of divine things. All those who are truly gracious persons have a solid, full, thorough and effectual conviction of the truth of the great things of the gospel. They no longer halt between two opinions; the great doctrines of the gospel cease to be any longer doubtful things, or matters of opinion, which, though probable, are yet disputable. Their eyes are opened so that they see that really Jesus is the Christ, the Son of the living God. That all true Christians have such a kind of conviction of the truth of the things of the gospel is abundantly manifest from the Holy Scriptures (Matt. 16:15-17; John 6:68-69; 17:6-8; Acts 8:37; II Cor. 4:11-14, 16, 18; 5:1, 6-8; I Tim. 1:12; Heb. 3:6; 11:1; I John 4:13-16; 5:4-5).

There are many religious affections which are not attended with such a conviction of the judgment. There are many apprehensions and ideas which some have, that they call divine discoveries, which are affecting but not convincing. Though they may seem to be persuaded, they have no thorough and effectual conviction. However great a show and noise they make, it is like the blaze of tow, or crackling of thorns. Some persons, under high affections, have that which they call a seeing the truth of the Word of God. Whereas the whole of their faith amounts to no more than only a strong confidence of their own good estate, and so a strong confidence that these words are true. Men may have a strong persuasion that the Christian religion is true, when their persuasion is not at all built on evidence, but altogether on education and the opinions of others. But if that belief of Christian doctrines, which persons' affections arise from, be truly gracious, it is requisite, not only that the belief should be reasonable, but also a spiritual belief or conviction. It is evident that there is such a thing as a spiritual belief or conviction of the things of the gospel, or a belief that is peculiar to those who are spiritual, and have the Spirit of God dwelling in them as a vital principle (Matt. 16:16-17, Luke 10: 21-22, John 16:27, 17:8, Gal. 1:14-16, II Cor. 4:3-6).

He that truly sees the divine, transcendent, supreme glory of those things which are divine, does as it were know their divinity intuitively. He not only argues that they are divine, but he sees that they are divine; not that he judges the doctrines of the gospel to be from God without any argument or deduction at all, but it is without any long chain of arguments; the argument is but one, and the evidence direct; the mind ascends the truth of the gospel but by one step, and that is its divine glory. Now the distinguishing glory of the divine Being has its brightest appearance in the things exhibited in the gospel, the doctrines taught, the divine counsels revealed. It is no argument that it cannot be seen, that some do not see it, though they may be discerning men in temporal matters. If there be such ineffable, distinguishing, evidential excellencies in the gospel, it is reasonable to suppose that they are such as are not to be discerned but by the special influence and enlightenings of the Spirit of God.

Sixth: Gracious affections are attended with evangelical humiliation; a sense that a Christian has of his own utter insufficiency, despicableness, and odiousness, with an answerable frame of heart.

There is a distinction to be made between a legal and evangelical humiliation. The former is from the common influence of the Spirit of God, assisting natural principles, and especially natural conscience; the latter is from the special influences of the Spirit of God, implanting and exercising supernatural and divine principles. In the former, men are made sensible that they are nothing before the great and terrible God, and wholly insufficient to help themselves: but they have not an answerable frame of heart, consisting in a disposition to abase themselves and exalt God alone. In the latter, they are brought sweetly to yield and freely to prostrate themselves at the feet of God. In legal humiliation the conscience is convinced; but because there is no spiritual understanding, the will is not bowed. Legal humiliation is useful as a means in order to evangelical, as a common knowledge of the things of religion is a means requisite in order to spiritual knowledge. But the essence of evangelical humiliation consists in such humility as becomes a creature under a dispensation of grace, consisting in a mean esteem of himself, attended with a mortification of a disposition to exalt himself, and a free renunciation of his own glory.

It concerns us greatly to look at this humiliation as one of the most essential things pertaining to true Christianity. They that are destitute of this, have no true religion, whatever profession they may make, and how high soever their religious affections may be (Hab. 2:4, Psa. 34:18, 51:17, Isa. 57:15, 66:1-2, Micah 6:8, Matt. 5:3, 18:3-4, Luke 18:9-14, Col. 3:12). There is a pretended great humiliation, and being emptied of self, which is one of the biggest and most elated things in the world. Some who think themselves quite emptied of themselves are full as they can hold with the glory of their own humility. Their humility is a swelling, self-conceited, confident, showy, noisy, assuming humility. For persons to be truly emptied of themselves, and to be poor in spirit, and broken in heart, is quite another thing, and has other effects than many imagine.

But though spiritual pride be so subtle an iniquity, and commonly appears under a pretext of great humility, yet there are two things by which it may (perhaps universally and surely) be discovered and distinguished. *First,* he that is under the prevalence of this distemper is apt to think highly of his attainments in religion, as comparing himself with others, (Luke 18:11, Isa. 65:5). And this may be laid down as an infallible thing, "That the person who is apt to think that he, as compared with others, is a very eminent saint, much distinguished in Christian experience, in whom this is a first thought, that rises of itself and naturally offers itself, he is certainly mistaken; he is no eminent saint, but under the great prevailings of a proud and self-righteous spirit." *Secondly,* another thing that is an infallible sign of spiritual pride is persons being apt to think highly of their humility. False experiences are commonly attended with a counterfeit humility, and it is the very nature of a counterfeit humility to be highly conceited of itself. The proud hypocrite is very often much in crying out of others' pride, finding fault with others' apparel and way of living. The humble Christian is a thousand times more quicksighted to discern his pride than his humility.

Seventh: Gracious affections are distinguished from others in that they are attended with a change of nature. The Scripture representations of conversion do strongly imply and signify a change of nature, such as "being born again, becoming new creatures, rising from the dead, being renewed in the spirit of the mind, putting off the old man and putting on the new."

Therefore, if there be no great and remarkable abiding change in persons that think they have experienced a work

of conversion, vain are all their imaginations and pre-
tences, however they have been affected. For in Christ
Jesus neither circumcision nor uncircumcision, neither
high profession nor low profession, neither a fair story
nor a broken one, avails anything; but a new creature.
If there be a very great alteration visible in a person for a
while, but he afterward returns to be much as he used to
be, it appears to be no change of nature, for nature is an
abiding thing. Indeed allowances must be made, for conversion does not entirely rout out natural temper. Those
sins which a man by his natural constitution was most
inclined to before his conversion, he may be most apt to
fall into still. Yet conversion will make a great alteration
even with respect to these sins. For God gives his Spirit
to be united to the faculties of soul, and to dwell after the
manner of a principle of nature. And a transformation of
nature is continued and carried on to the end of life, until
it is brought to perfection in glory. Hence the progress
of the work of grace in the hearts of the saints is represented in Scripture as a continued conversion and reno-
vation of nature (Rom. 12:2, Eph. 4:22-24).

Eighth: Truly gracious affections naturally beget and
promote such a spirit of love, meekness, quietness, forgiveness and mercy, as appeared in Christ. It is the spirit
by which real disciples of Christ are possessed and governed, their true and proper character (Matt. 5:5, 7, 9;
Col. 3:12-13; Cor. 13:4-5; Gal. 5:22-23; James 3:14-17).

There are some amiable qualities and virtues that especially agree with the nature of the gospel constitution and
Christian profession, such as humility, meekness, love,
forgiveness, and mercy. These things are spoken of as what
are especially the character of Jesus Christ himself (Matt.
21:5, 11:29). The same appears by the name which
Christ is so often called in Scripture, viz. the Lamb. So

Christians are Christlike. Meekness is so much the character of the saints that the meek and the godly are used as synonymous terms in Scripture (II Cor. 3:18, I Cor. 15:47-49, 6:17, Luke 10:3, Psa. 37:10-11, 147:6).

Here some are ready to say, Is there no such thing as Christian fortitude and boldness for Christ? There doubtless is such a thing. The whole Christian life is compared to a warfare, and fitly so. Yet many persons seem to be quite mistaken concerning the nature of Christian fortitude. When persons are fierce and violent, and exert their bitter passions, it shows weakness instead of strength. True Christian fortitude consists in strength of mind, through grace, exerted in two things: in ruling and suppressing the evil and unruly passions and affections of the mind; and in following good affections and dispositions without being hindered by sinful fear or the opposition of enemies.

The Scripture knows of no true Christians as are of a sordid, selfish, cross and contentious spirit. Nothing can be invented that is a greater absurdity than a morose, hard, close, high-spirited, spiteful true Christian. We must learn the way of bringing men to rules, and not rules to men and so strain and stretch the rules of God's Word, to take in ourselves and some of our neighbors, until we make them wholly of none effect.

Ninth: Gracious affections soften the heart, and are attended and followed with a Christian tenderness of spirit. They turn a heart of stone more and more into a heart of flesh.

False affections, however persons may seem to be melted by them while they are new, yet have a tendency in the end to harden the heart. A disposition to some kind of passions may be established, such as self-seeking, self-exaltation, and opposition to others. False affections, with the delusion that attends them, finally tend to stupify the mind. And the effect at last is that persons in the settled frame of their minds become less affected with their present and past sins and less conscientious with respect to their future sins.

Tenth: In the true holy affections of the saints is found a proportion which is the natural consequence of their sanctification. Not that the symmetry of the virtues of the saints in this life is perfect. It often is defective through errors in judgment or defects in education, and many other disadvantages that might be mentioned. Yet there is in no wise that monstrous disproportion that is commonly to be observed in the false religion and counterfeit graces of hypocrites.

It is with hypocrites as with Ephraim of old, "Ephraim is a cake not turned," (Hosea 7:8), half roasted and half raw. There is no manner of uniformity in their affections. There is also often a strange partiality in the same affections with regard to different objects. Thus some make high pretenses and a great show of love to God, but they have not a spirit of love towards men. And as to love to men, it is far from being so extensive and universal as a Christian love is. They are full of dear affections to some, and full of bitterness towards others (Matt. 5:45-46). Some are liberal of their worldly substance, and give to the poor, but have no love for the souls of men. Others pretend a great love to men's souls, that are not compassionate and charitable towards their bodies. And some persons seem to be much affected with the bad qualities of their fellow Christians, but are in no proportion affected with their own defects. And here, by the way, I would observe that it may be laid down as a general rule, that if persons pretend that they come to high attainments in religion, but have never yet arrived to the less attainments, it is a sign of vain pretense.

As there is a disproportion in the exercises of false affections as to different objects, so there is also as to different times. If persons are religious only by fits and starts, now raised up to the clouds and then suddenly down again, or suppose that they are newly converted but quickly their hearts are chiefly upon other things, it is a sign of the unsoundness of their affections. And as there is a strange unevenness in false affections at different times, so there often is in different places. Some are greatly affected when in company, but have nothing when alone and separated from all the world. True religion disposes persons to be much alone in solitary places for meditation and prayer.

Eleventh: Another distinguishing difference between gracious affections and others is that gracious affections, the higher they are raised the more is a spiritual appetite and longing of soul after spiritual attainments increased. On the contrary, false affections rest satisfied in themselves (Phil. 3:13-15).

Here some may object, How is this consistent with what all allow, that spiritual enjoyments are said to be of a soul-satisfying nature? I answer, Spiritual enjoyments are of a soul-satisfying nature in the following respects: (1) They, in the kind and nature, are fully adapted to the nature, capacity, and need of the soul of man. (2) They answer the expectation of the appetite. (3) The gratification of spiritual enjoyments is permanent. But these things do not argue that a soul has no appetite excited after more of the same that has tasted a little; or that his appetite will not increase, the more he tastes, until he comes to full enjoyment. The Scriptures everywhere represent the seeking, striving, and labor of a Christian as being chiefly after his conversion, and his conversion as being but the beginning of his work.

Twelfth: Gracious and holy affections have their exercise and fruit in Christian practice. This implies three things.

(1) That the Christian's behavior or practice in this world be universally conformed to, and directed by, Christian rules. It is necessary that men be obedient (I John 3:3ff, 5:18, John 15:14, Matt. 5:29-30, Num. 14:24). And it is important that a man's obedience not only consist in negatives, or in avoiding wicked practices, but he must also be universal in the positives of religion (Matt. 25: 31-46). So it is necessary that men should part with their dearest iniquities, and obey the law of Christ that he and his apostles did insist on.

(2) In order to men's being true Christians, it is necessary that they prosecute religion as the main business of their lives (Tit. 2:14; Phil. 3:13; Matt. 25:26, 30; Heb. 6:11-12; 12:1; typified Ex. 12:11). Slothfulness in the service of God in his professed servants is as damning as open rebellion.

(3) Every true Christian perseveres in this way of universal obedience, and earnest service, to the end of life (Deut. 5:29; I Chron. 28:9; Psa. 106:3, 12-15; Isa. 64:5; Ezek. 18:24; Matt. 10:22; 13:4-8; Luke 9:62; 12:35ff; John 8:30-31; Rom 2:7; 11:22; Col. 1:22-23; etc.). Christ is not in the heart of a saint as a dead Saviour that does nothing. In the heart where Christ is, there he lives, and exerts himself after the power of that endless life that he received at his resurrection. Hence saving affections, though oftentimes they do not make so great a noise and show as others, yet have in them a secret solidity, life, and strength, gaining a full and steadfast determination of the will for God and holiness (II Cor. 10:5).

What makes men partial in religion is that they seek themselves and not God; and close with religion, not for its own excellent nature, but only to serve a turn. He that closes with religion only to serve a turn, will close with no more of it than he imagines serves that turn. He that embraces religion for its own sake, embraces the whole of it. Religion may alter greatly in process of time, as to its consistence with men's private interest; and therefore he that complies with it only for selfish views, is liable in change of times to forsake it. But the excellent nature of religion is invariable; it is the same at all times and through all changes; it never alters in any respect. And our heart's entirely closing with the religion of Jesus, upon a deliberate counting of the cost, tends to a universal closing with the same in act and deed. And actually going through all the difficulties we meet with patience and perseverance.

Christian practice, or a holy life, is a great and distinguishing sign of true and saving grace. I may go farther and assert that it is the chief of all the signs of grace. But then it is necessary that this be rightly understood, in what sense and manner Christian practice is the greatest sign of grace. I will endeavor to set the matter in a clear light.

(a) Christian practice is the sign of the sincerity of a professing Christian to the eye of his neighbors and brethren. This is evident from the Word of God. "Ye shall know them by their fruits" (Matt. 7:16, 20; 12:33; Luke 6:44; Heb. 6:9-10; III John 3-6; James 2:18). And as Scripture plainly teaches that practice is the best evidence of the sincerity of professing Christians, so reason teaches the same thing. Men's deeds are better and more faithful interpreters of their minds than their words. If a man appears to walk humbly before God and men, this is a better evidence of humiliation than if a person only tells how great a sense he had of his own unworthiness, but yet acts as if he looked upon himself as one of the best of saints. Passing affections easily produce words, and words are cheap, and godliness is more easily feigned in words than in actions. Christian practice is a costly, laborious thing.

It must be observed that a profession of Christianity is not excluded, but supposed. Profession of Christianity is requisite. If any man should say plainly that he was not a Christian, Christ and his apostles do not at all oblige us to look upon him as a sincere Christian, let his visible practice and virtues be what they will. Moreover, that profession which is properly called a Christian profession, and which must be joined with Christian practice, must be made understandingly. That is, persons must appear to have been so far instructed in the principles of religion as to be in an ordinary capacity to understand what is the proper import of what is expressed in their profession. There ought to be good reason to think that the professor does not make such a profession out of a mere customary compliance with a prescribed form, or in a very lax and ambiguous manner, as confessions of faith are often subscribed.

(b) The Scripture also speaks of Christian practice as a distinguishing and sure evidence of grace to persons' own consciences (I John 3:18-19, Heb. 6:9, Gal. 6:4, Matt. 7:19-29). Here I would observe that we cannot reasonably suppose that when the Scripture in this case speaks of good works, it has respect merely to what is external, having no respect to any aim or intention of the agent, or any act of his understanding or will. For consider men's actions so, and they are no more good works or acts of obedience than the regular motions of a clock. But the obedience and fruit that is spoken of, is the obedience of the soul, consisting in the acts and practice of the soul. Not that I suppose, when Scripture speaks in this case, that in these expressions are included all inward piety and holiness of heart, both principle and exercise, both spirit and practice: because then the same thing would be given as a sign of itself, and there would be no distinction between root and fruit. Only the gracious exercise and holy act of the soul is meant, the practical exertion in inward holiness which there is in an obediential act, in which something is directed and commanded by the soul to be done, and brought to pass in practice. Would anybody call the voluntary actions of a man, externally and materially agreeable to a command of Christ, by the name of obedience to Christ, if he had never heard of Christ or had no thought of his commands in what he did? As God looks at the obedience and practice of the man, he looks at the practice of the soul; for the soul is the man in God's sight, "for the Lord seeth not as man seeth, for he looketh on the heart." Thus when practice is given in Scripture as the main evidence to others of our true Christianity, then is meant *that* in our practice which is visible to them. But when practice is given as a sure evidence of our real Christianity to our own consciences, then is meant *that* in our practice which is visible to our own consciences (Matt. 5:3,4,7,8; John 13:34-35; 15:10, 12-14; II John 5-6; Rev. 2:23; Jer. 17:9-10; Isa. 38:3).

Christian practice, taken in the sense that has been explained, is the chief of all the evidences of a saving sincerity in religion to the consciences of the professors of it. Reason plainly shows that what men will actually cleave to and prefer in practice, when left to follow their own choice and inclinations, is the proper trial of the sincerity of their hearts. Sincerity in religion consists in setting God highest in the heart, forsaking all for Christ;

but to forsake all for Christ in the heart is the very same thing as to have a heart to forsake all for Christ. It is absurd for any to pretend they have a good heart while they live a wicked life (Deut. 5:27-29, Gal. 6:7). The things that put to the proof whether men will prefer God to other things in practice, are those which occur that make the practice of duty difficult. Hereby professors are proved what sort they be (Judg. 2:21-22, I Pet. 1:6-7, II Cor. 8:8, Psa. 66:10-11, Zech. 13:9). This is the grand evidence which will hereafter be made use of before the judgment seat of God. God's future judging of men to their eternal retribution will not be his trying and passing a judgment upon the state of men's hearts, in his own mind; it will be a declarative judgment.   And the end of it will be the righteousness of his judgment to men's own consciences, and to the world (Rom. 2:5; Matt. 18:31-35, 20:8-15; 25:19-30, 35-46; Luke 19:15-23; Rev. 20:12-13; II Cor. 5:10).

Now from all that has been said, I think it to be abundantly manifest that Christian practice is the most proper evidence of the gracious sincerity of professors, to themselves and to others, the chief of all the marks of grace, the sign of signs, and evidence of evidences. Practice is the proper proof of the true and saving knowledge of God Titus 1:16, John 13:17, Rom. 1:21), the proper evidence of repentance, of a saving faith and of a saving belief of the truth (James 2:21-24, III John 3), the proper evidence of a true coming to Christ, of a gracious love both to God and men (Micah 6:8), of true thankfulness (Psa. 116:12), of a gracious hope (I John 3:3, I Pet. 1:13-14), and of Christian fortitude (I Cor. 9:25-26, II Tim. 2:3-5).

Before I conclude this discourse I would answer briefly

two objections that may possibly be made by some against what has been said.

Objection I. This seems to be contrary to that opinion so much received among good people; that professors should judge of their state chiefly by their inward experience and that spiritual experiences are the main evidence of true grace.

The chief sign of grace to the consciences of Christians, being Christian practice, is not at all inconsistent with Christian experience being the chief evidence of grace. Spiritual practice in man is the practice of a spirit and body jointly, or the practice of a spirit animating, commanding and actuating a body to which it is united. And therefore the main thing in this holy practice is the holy action of the mind, directing and governing the motions of the body. Christian experience consists as much in those operative exercises of grace in the will, that are immediately concerned in the management of the behavior of the body, as in other exercises. To speak of Christian experience and practice as if they were two things, properly and entirely distinct, is to make a distinction without consideration or reason. Indeed, all Christian experience is not properly called practice, but all Christian practice is properly experience. And the distinction that is made between them is not only unreasonable but unscriptural (Jer. 22:15, 16; I John 5:3; II John 6; Psa. 34:11-14; II Cor. 1:12; 4:13; 5:7; 6:47; Gal. 2:20; Phil. 3:78; Col. 1:29; II Thess. 2:2, 8-10; II Tim. 4:6-7).

Objection II. Some may object that this making of Christian practice the chief evidence of the truth of grace is a legal doctrine, to the diminution of the glory of free grace and the great gospel doctrine of justification by faith alone.

This objection is altogether without reason. It is our works being the price of God's favor, and not their being the sign of it, that is inconsistent with the freeness of that favor. The freeness of the grace of God to sinners is not that no holy qualifications or actions in us shall be a fruit, and so a sign of that grace; but that it is not the worthiness of any qualification or action of ours which recommends us to that grace. It would be legal to suppose that holy practice justifies by bringing us to a title to Christ's benefits; but it is not legal to suppose that holy practice justifies the sincerity of a believer as the proper evidence of it. So the freeness of grace and the necessity of holy practice are not inconsistent with one another. It is greatly to the hurt of religion to neglect the effectual operations of grace in practice, and insist almost wholly on the manner of the exercises of conscience in contemplation.

It is our wisdom not to take God's work out of his hands, but to follow him where he has directed us. Thus the light of professors would so shine before men that others, seeing their good works, would glorify their Father which is in heaven.

The Treatise on Grace *

(A) Such phrases as *common grace,* and *special* or *saving grace,* may be understood as signifying either diverse kinds of influence of God's Spirit on the hearts of men, or diverse fruits and effects of that influence. Sometimes the phrase common grace is used to signify that kind of action or influence of the Spirit of God, to which are owing those religious or moral attainments that are common to both saints and sinners, and so signifies as much as common assistance: and sometimes those moral or religious attainments themselves, as the fruits of this assistance are intended. So likewise the phrase *special* or *saving* grace is sometimes used to signify that peculiar kind or degree of operation or influence of God's Spirit, whence saving actions and attainments do arise in the godly, or, which is the same thing, special and saving assistance; or else to signify that distinguishing saving virtue itself, which is the fruit of this assistance. These phrases are more frequently understood in the latter sense, viz., not for common and special assistance, but for common and special or saving virtue, which is the fruit of that assistance, and so I would be understood by these phrases in this discourse.

* Editor's note: *The Treatise on Grace* is not condensed in its entirety here, but rather those portions have been chosen from it which throw light on Edwards' thinking with regard to "conversion." This treatise contains many of the same thoughts which are in the treatise on Religious Affections. There is little point in repeating these, and only such material is here printed as will lend additional light to what has already been given.

And that special or saving grace in this sense is not only different from common grace in degree, but entirely diverse in nature and kind, and that natural men not only have not a sufficient degree of virtue to be saints, but that they have no degree of that grace that is in godly men, is what I have now to show.

(1) This is evident by what Christ says in John 3:6; Gal. 5:17, 19, 22; 6:8; Rom. 8:6-9; I Cor. 3:1.

(2) That principle in those that are savingly converted, whence gracious acts flow, which in the language of Scripture is called the spirit, and set in opposition to the flesh, is that which others not only have not a sufficient degree of, but have nothing at all of, Rom. 8:9, I John 3:24.

(3) Those that are not true saints, and in a state of salvation, not only have not so much of that holy nature and divine principle that is in the hearts of the saints but they do not partake of it, because a being "partakers of the divine nature" is spoken of as the peculiar privilege of true saints, II Pet. 1:4.

(4) That those who are not true saints have no degree of that grace that the saints have is evident, because they have no communion or fellowship with Christ. There is no communion without union, John 1:16.

(5) This is confirmed by the things that conversion is represented by in the Scriptures, particularly its being represented as a work of creation. When God creates he does not merely establish and perfect the things which were made before, but makes wholly and immediately something entirely new, either out of nothing, or out of that which was perfectly void of any such nature.

Inference 1. From what has been said, I would observe that it must needs be that conversion is wrought at once.

That knowledge, that reformation and conviction that is preparatory to conversion may be gradual, and the work of grace after conversion may be gradually carried on, yet that work of grace upon the soul whereby a person is brought out of a state of total corruption and depravity into a state of grace, to an interest in Christ, and to be actually a child of God, is in a moment.

Those things by which conversion is represented in Scripture hold forth the same thing. In creation something is brought out of nothing in an instant, Rom. 8:28-20, Acts 2:37-39, I Thess. 5:23-24, etc. Conversion, in Scripture, is often compared to resurrection. Thus it is said, "If any man be in Christ, he is a new creature," which obviously implies that he is an exceeding diverse kind of creature from what he was before he was in Christ, that the principles or qualities that he has by which he is a Christian are entirely new, and what there was nothing of, before he was in Christ.

Inference 2. Hence we may learn that it is impossible for men to convert themselves by their own strength and industry. Saving grace in the heart can not be produced in man by mere exercise of what perfections he has in him already. Grace must be the immediate work of God, and properly a production of his almighty power on the soul.

(B) Showing wherein all saving grace does summarily consist.

(1) That saving grace that is in the hearts of the saints, and entirely distinguishes them from all unconverted men, is radically but one — i.e., however various its exercises are, yet is but one in its root; it is one individual principle in the heart.

(2) That principle in the soul of the saints which is the grand Christian virtue, and which is the soul and es

sence and summary comprehension of all grace, *is a principle of divine love.* This is evident because:

(a) We are abundantly taught in the Scripture that divine love is the sum of all duty, Rom. 13:8, I Tim. 1:5.

(b) The apostle speaks of divine love as that which is the essence of all Christianity in the thirteenth chapter of the First Epistle to the Corinthians.

That love to God and a Christian love to men are thus but one in their root and foundation-principle in the heart is confirmed by several passages in the First Epistle of John, 3:16-17, 4:20-21, 5:1-2. Divine love, as it has God for its object, may thus be described. It is the soul's relish of the supreme excellency of the divine nature, including the heart to God as the chief good.

(C) Showing how a principle of grace is from the Spirit of God.

(1) That this holy and divine principle, which we have shown does radically and summarily consist in divine love, comes into existence in the soul by the power of God in the influences of the Holy Spirit, the Third Person in the Trinity, is abundantly manifest from the Scriptures. Regeneration is by the Spirit, John 3:5-6. The renewing of the soul is by the Holy Ghost, Titus 3:5; Ezek. 36:26, 27; John 6:63; etc. This doctrine of a gracious nature being by the immediate influence of the Spirit of God, is not only taught in the Scriptures, but is irrefragable to reason.

(2) The Scripture speaks of this holy and divine principle in the heat as not only from the Spirit, but as being spiritual. Concerning this, two things are to be noted.

(a) This divine principle is called spiritual, not because of its relation to the spirit of man, in which it is, but because of its relation to the Spirit of God, from which it is.

(b) It must be observed that where this holy divine principle of saving grace wrought in the mind is in Scripture called spiritual, what is intended by the expression is not merely nor chiefly that it is from the Spirit of God, but that it is of the nature of the Spirit of God.

The Holy Spirit does in some ineffable and inconceivable manner proceed, and is breathed forth both from the Father and the Son, by the divine essence being wholly poured and flowing out in that infinitely intense, holy and pure love and delight that continually and unchangeably breathes forth from the Father and the Son. The Holy Ghost is that love of God and Christ that is breathed forth primarily towards each other, and secondarily towards the creature.

Both the holiness and happiness of the Godhead consists in this love. As we have already proved, all creature holiness consists essentially and summarily in love to God and love to other creatures; so does the holiness of God consist in his love, especially in the perfect and intimate union and love there is between the Father and the Son. Hence we may better understand the economy of the Persons of the Trinity as it appears in the part that each one has in the affair of redemption, and the equality of honor and praise due to each of them.

Judging Persons' Experiences *

Directions For Judging of Persons' Experiences

SEE TO IT:

That the operation be much upon the will or heart, not on the imagination nor on the speculative understanding, or motions of the mind, though they draw great affections after them as the consequence.

That the trouble of mind be reasonable, that the mind be troubled about those things that it has reason to be troubled about; and that the trouble seems mainly to operate in such a manner, with such a kind of trouble and exercise, as is reasonable: founded on reasonable, solid consideration; a solid sense and conviction of truth, as of things as they are indeed.

That it be because their state appears terrible on the account of those things, wherein its dreadfulness indeed consists; and that their concern be solid, not operating very much by pangs and sudden passions, freaks and frights, and a capriciousness of mind.

That they be convinced of sins of heart and life: that their pretenses of sense of sin of heart be not without reflection of their wicked practice; and also that they are not only convinced of sin of practice, but sin of heart.

* Editor's note: Edwards apparently used a sort of guide in his test-conversations when any one came to inquire of him, or get his opinion, during The Great Awakening, or Revivals. Only some of his points are printed here, the ones which are in part repetitious having been omitted.

And in both, that what troubles them be those things wherein their wretchedness chiefly consisted.

That they are convinced of their spiritual sins, consisting in their sinful defects, living without love to God, and without accepting Christ, gratitude to him, etc.

That God and divine things are admirable on account of the beauty of their moral perfection.

That there is to be discerned in their sense of the sufficiency of Christ a sense of that divine, supreme, and spiritual excellency of Christ, wherein this sufficiency fundamentally consists; and that the sight of this excellency is really the foundation of their satisfaction as to his sufficiency.

That they long after *holiness*, and that all their experiences increase their longing.

Let them be inquired of concerning their disposition and willingness to bear the cross, sell all for Christ, choosing their portion in heaven, etc.

Inquire whether their joy be truly and properly in God and in Christ, joy in divine good; or whether it be not wholly joy in themselves, joy in their own excellencies or privileges, in their experiences, what God has done for them, or what he has promised he will do for them; and whether they be not affected with their own discoveries and affections.

Sinners in the Hands of an Angry God

*A Sermon Preached at Enfield, July 8th, 1741, at
a Time of Great Awakening.*

Text: *Deut.* 32:35. *". . . their foot shall slide in due
time . . . ."*

Introduction: In this verse is threatened the vengeance
of God on the wicked unbelieving Israelites, that were God's
people, and lived under means of grace; and that notwithstanding all God's wonderful works, yet remained (as expressed in verse 28) void of counsel, having no understanding in them.

The expression I have chosen for my text seems to
imply the following:

(a) They were always exposed to destruction, as one
that stands or walks in slippery places is always exposed
to fall. The same is expressed in Psa. 73:18.

(b) They were always exposed to sudden unexpected
destruction. As he that walks in slippery places, when
he does fall, falls at once without warning. Also Psa.
73:18-19.

(c) They are liable to fall of themselves, without being
thrown down by the hand of another.

(d) The reason they are not fallen already is only that
God's appointed time is not come. When that time comes,
their foot shall slide; God will not hold them up in these
slippery places any longer.

Observation: The observation from the words that I would now insist upon is this, "There is nothing that keeps wicked men at any one moment out of hell, but the mere pleasure of God." I mean his sovereign pleasure, restrained by no obligation, hindered by no manner of difficulty.

Considerations: The truth of this observation may appear by the following considerations.

(1) There is no want of power in God to cast wicked men into hell at any moment. There is no fortress that is any defense from the power of God. God's enemies are easily broken in pieces. They are as great heaps of light chaff before the whirlwind, or large quantities of dry stubble before devouring flames. It is easy for us to cut or singe a single slender thread that any thing hangs by; thus it is easy for God, when he pleases, to cast his enemies down to hell.

(2) They deserve to be cast into hell. The sword of divine justice is every moment brandished over their heads, and it is nothing but the hand of arbitrary mercy, and God's will, that holds it back.

(3) They are already under a sentence of condemnation to hell. The sentence of the law of God, that eternal and immutable rule of righteousness that God has fixed between him and mankind, stands against them, John 3:18, 8:23.

(4) They are now the objects of that very same anger and wrath of God that is expressed in the torments of hell. As angry as God is with many of those miserable creatures that now feel and bear the fierceness of his wrath, God is a great deal more angry with great numbers that are now on earth, yea, doubtless, that are now in this congregation. The wrath of God burns against them; their

damnation does not slumber; the fire is made ready; the furnace is now hot.

(5) The devil stands ready to fall upon them, and seize them as his own, at what moment God shall permit him. They belong to him; he has their souls in his possesion, and under his dominion, Luke 11:21. If God should permit it, they would be hastily swallowed up and lost.

(6) There are in the souls of wicked men those hellish principles reigning that would presently flame out into hell fire, if it were not for God's restraints. These principles are active and powerful, exceeding violent in their nature. The souls of the wicked are in Scripture compared to the troubled sea, (Isa. 57:20). For the present God restrains their wickedness by his mighty power; but if he should withdraw that restraining power, it would soon carry all before it. Sin is the ruin and misery of the soul; it is destructive in its nature; and if God should leave it without restraint, there would need nothing else to make the soul perfectly miserable. The corruption of the heart of man is a thing that is immoderate and boundless in its fury.

(7) It is no security to wicked men that there are no visible means of death at hand. It is no security to a natural man that he is now in health, that he does not see which way he should now immediately go out of the world by an accident. Unconverted men walk over the pit of hell on a rotten covering. There is nothing to make it appear that God had need to be at the expense of a miracle to destroy any wicked man, at any moment.

(8) Natural men's care to preserve their own lives, or the care of others to preserve them, do not secure them for a moment. "How dieth the wise man? as the fool," Eccles. 2:16.

(9) All men's contrivances they use to escape hell, while they continue to reject Christ, do not secure them from hell one moment. Almost every natural man that hears of hell flatters himself that he shall escape it; he depends upon himself for his own security; he flatters himself in what he has done, in what he is now doing, or what he intends to do. They hear that there are but few saved, but each one imagines that he lays out matters better for his own escape than others have done. But the foolish children of men miserably delude themselves in their own schemes, and in their confidence in their own strength and wisdom; they trust nothing but a shadow.

(10) God has laid himself under no obligation to keep any natural man out of hell one moment. God has made no promises either of eternal life, or of any deliverance from eternal death, but what are contained in the covenant of grace, the promises that are given in Christ. So it is plain that whatever pains a natural man takes in religion, whatever prayer he makes, till he believes in Christ, God is under no obligation to keep him a moment from eternal destruction.

So that thus it is that natural men are held in the hand of God over the pit of hell; they have deserved the fiery pit, and are already sentenced to it. The devil is waiting for them, hell is gaping for them. They have no refuge. All that preserves them is the mere arbitrary will, and un-covenanted, unobliged forbearance of an incensed God.

Application: This that you have heard is the case of every one of you that is out of Christ. You have nothing to stand upon, nor anything to take hold of. There is nothing between you and hell but the air; it is only the power and mere pleasure of God that holds you up. You probably are not sensible of this; you find you are kept out of hell, but you do not see the hand of God in it.

Were it not that so is the sovereign pleasure of God, the earth would not bear you one moment, for you are a burden to it. The creation groans with you; the creature is made subject to the bondage of your corruption, not willingly; the sun does not willingly shine upon you to give you light to serve sin; the earth does not willingly yield her increases to satisfy your lusts. God's creatures are good, and were made for men to serve God with, and groan when they are abused to purposes so directly contrary to their nature and end. And the world would spew you out, were it not for the sovereign hand of him who hath subjected it in hope.

There are black clouds of God's wrath now hanging directly over your heads, full of the dreadful storm. The sovereign pleasure of God for the present stays the rough wind, otherwise your destruction would come like a whirlwind. The wrath of God is like great waters that are dammed up for the present. The bow of God's wrath is bent; and justice bends the arrow at your heart, and strains the bow; and it is nothing but the mere pleasure of God that keeps the arrow.

Thus are all you that never passed under a great change of heart by the mighty power of the Spirit of God upon your souls, all that were never born again and made new creatures (however you may have reformed your life in many things, and may have religious affections, and may keep a form of religion, and may be strict in it). The God that holds you over the pit of hell, much as one holds a spider over the fire, is dreadfully provoked; his wrath toward you burns like fire. It is nothing but his hand that keeps you from falling into the fire every moment. O sinner! Consider the fearful danger you are in: you hang by a slender thread with the flames of divine wrath flashing about it, ready every moment to singe it, and burn it asunder; and you have nothing you have ever done to induce God to spare you one moment.

Consider more particularly several things concerning that wrath you are in such danger of.

(a) Whose wrath it is. If it were only the wrath of man, though the most potent prince, it would be comparatively little to be regarded. But the greatest earthly potentates are but feeble in comparison of the almighty Creator of heaven and earth. The wrath of the great King of kings is as much more terrible than theirs, as his majesty is greater (Luke 12:4-5).

(b) It is the fierceness of his wrath that you are exposed to. We often read of the fury of God, Isa. 59:18, 66:15, Rev. 19:15. We can conceive what such expressions carry in them! To what a dreadful, inexpressible depth of misery must the poor creature sink who shall be the subject of this!

Consider this, you that are present, that yet remain in an unregenerate state. Now God stands ready to pity you; this is a day of mercy; you may cry now with some encouragement of obtaining mercy. But when once the day of mercy is past, your most lamentable cries will be in vain (Ezek. 8:18); you will be wholly lost and thrown away of God, as to any regard of your welfare. How awful are the words of Isa. 63:3, "I will tread them in mine anger, and trample them in my fury, and their blood shall be sprinkled upon my garments . . . ." It is perhaps impossible to conceive of words that carry in them greater contempt and hatred, and fierceness of indignation.

(c) The misery which God will inflict to that end. God hath had it on his heart to show both how excellent his love is, and also how terrible his wrath is. God is willing to show his wrath, and magnify his awful majesty and mighty power in the extreme suffering of his enemies (Rom. 9:22, Isa. 33:12-14).

(d) It is everlasting wrath. It would be dreadful to suffer this fierceness and wrath of Almighty God one moment; but you must suffer it to all eternity. When you look forward, you shall see a boundless duration before you, and you will despair of ever having any deliverance. Oh, who can express what the state of a soul in such circumstances is!

Conclusion: This is the dismal case of every soul in this congregation that has not been born again. Oh, that you would consider it, whether you be young or old.

If we knew that but one person in the whole congregation was to be the subject of this misery, what an awful thing would it be to think of! How might all the rest of the congregation lift up a lamentable and bitter cry over him! But alas! Instead of one, how many is it likely will remember this discourse in hell? And it would be a wonder if some that are present should not be in hell in a very short time, before the year is out. And it would be no wonder if some persons that now sit here in health and quiet, and secure, should be there tomorrow morning.

Reality of Spiritual Light

A Divine and Supernatural Light, Immediately imparted to the Soul by the Spirit of God, Shown to be both a Scriptural and Rational Doctrine.

Text: Matt. 16:17. *"And Jesus answered and said unto him, Blessed art thou, Simon Barjona: for flesh and blood hath not revealed it unto thee, but my Father which is in heaven."*

Introduction: Christ says these words to Peter upon occasion of his professing his faith in him as the Son of God. Our Lord was inquiring of his disciples who men said he was; not that he needed to be informed, but only to introduce and give occasion to what follows. Simon Peter, whom we find always zealous and forward, was the first to answer: "Thou art Christ, the Son of the living God."

Upon this occasion Christ says to him, and of him, the text in which we may observe:

(1) That Peter is pronounced blessed on this account. "Thou art a happy man, that thou art not ignorant of this, that I am Christ, the Son of the living God."

(2) The evidence of this his happiness declared; viz., that God, and he only, had revealed it to him. This is an evidence of his being blessed. It shows how favored he was of God above others. Also, it intimates that this knowledge is above any that flesh and blood can reveal.

God is the author of all knowledge and understanding whatsoever. He is the author of the knowledge that is obtained by human learning, but yet not so but that flesh and blood reveal it. Mortal men are capable of imparting

130

the knowledge of human arts and sciences, and skill in temporal affairs. God is the author of such knowledge by those means: flesh and blood is made use of by God as the mediate or second cause of it; he conveys it by the power and influence of natural means. But this spiritual knowledge, spoken of in the text, is what God is the author of, and none else. He reveals it, and flesh and blood reveals it not. He imparts this knowledge immediately, not making use of any intermediate natural causes, as he does in other knowledge. This could be owing only to the gracious distinguishing influence and revelation of the Spirit of God.

Doctrine: That there is such a thing as a spiritual and divine light, immediately imparted to the soul by God, of a different nature from any that is obtained by natural means.

(I) I would show what this spiritual and divine light is.

(A) In order to it, first in a few things what it is not.

(1) Those convictions that natural men have of their sin and misery is not this spiritual and divine light. Men in a natural condition may have convictions of the guilt that lies upon them. And this light and conviction may be from the Spirit of God. But it is from the Spirit of God only as assisting natural principles, and not as infusing any new principles. Conscience is a principle natural to men; and the work that it doth naturally is to give an apprehension of right and wrong, and to suggest to the mind the relation there is between right and wrong, and a retribution. The Spirit of God, in those convictions which unregenerate men sometimes have, assists conscience to do this work in a further degree than it would do if they were left to themselves.

The Spirit of God acts in a very different manner in the one case from what he doth in another. He may indeed act upon the mind of a natural man but he acts in the mind of a saint as an indwelling principle. He acts upon the mind of an unregenerate person as an extrinsic, occasional agent; but he unites himself with the mind of a saint and influences him as a new supernatural principle.

(2) This spiritual and divine light does not consist in any impression made upon the imagination. It is no impression upon mind, as though one saw anything with the bodily eyes. The imagination may be strongly impressed, but this is not spiritual light. We cannot determine but that the devil, who transforms himself into an angel of light, may cause imaginations of an outward beauty, or visible glory, and of sounds and speeches, and other such things, but these are of a vastly inferior nature to spiritual light.

(3) This spiritual light is not the suggesting of any new truths or propositions not contained in the Word of God. This suggesting of new truths, independent of any antecedent revelation, is inspiration, such as the apostles and prophets had, and such as some enthusiasts pretend to. But this spiritual light that I am speaking of is quite a different thing from inspiration. It reveals no new doctrine, it suggests no new proposition to the mind not taught in the Bible, but only gives a due apprehension of those things that are taught in the Word of God.

(4) It is not every affecting view that men have of the things of religion that is this spiritual and divine light. Men by mere principles of nature are capable of being affected with things that have a special relation to religion, for instance, the story of Jesus, and the sufferings he underwent. We read in Scripture of many that were greatly affected with things of a religious nature, who yet are there represented as wholly graceless. A person therefore

may have affecting views of the things of religion, and yet be very destitute of spiritual light.

(B) I proceed to show positively what this spiritual and divine light is. And it may be described thus: A true sense of the divine excellency of the things revealed in the Word of God, and a conviction of the truth and reality of them thence arising.

(1) There is in this spiritual light a true sense of the divine and superlative excellency of the things of religion; a real sense of the excellency of God and Jesus Christ, and of the work of redemption, and the ways and works of God revealed in the gospel. There is not only a rational belief that God is holy, but there is a sense of the loveliness of God's holiness.

There is a difference between having an opinion that God is holy and gracious, and having a sense of the loveliness and beauty of that holiness and grace. There is a difference between having a rational judgment that honey is sweet, and having a sense of its sweetness. A man may have the former that knows not how honey tastes, but a man cannot have the latter unless he has an idea of the taste of honey in his mind. The former rests only in the head, but the heart is concerned in the latter.

(2) There arises from this sense of divine excellency of things contained in the Word of God a conviction of the truth and reality of them. Indirectly the prejudices that are in the heart against divine things are hereby removed. Hence the different effect that Christ's miracles had to convince the disciples from what they had to convince the Scribes and Pharisees. Not that they had a stronger reason, but their reason was sanctified and those blinding prejudices removed. Reason itself is under far greater advantages for its proper and free exercise, free from darkness and delusion.

This evidence, that the spiritually enlightened have of the truth of the things of religion, is a kind of intuitive and immediate evidence. They believe the doctrines of God's Word to be divine because they see divinity in them. Such a conviction of the truth of religion as this is that true spiritual conviction that there is in a saving faith.

(II) I proceed now to the second thing proposed, viz., to show how this light is immediately given by God, and not obtained by natural means.

(A) It is not intended that the natural faculties are not made use of in it. They are not merely passive, but active in it. Yet this light is not the less immediately from God for that. The faculties are made use of as the subject and not as the cause, as the use that we make of our eyes in beholding objects is not the cause of the light that discovers those objects to us.

(B) This light is given immediately by God without making use of any means that operate by their own power, or a natural force. God makes use of means, but it is not as mediate causes to produce this effect. There are not truly any secondary causes; it is produced by God immediately. The Word of God is only made use of to convey to the mind the subject matter of this saving instruction. The notions that are the subject matter of his light are conveyed to the mind by the Word of God; but that due sense of the heart, wherein this light formally consists, is immediately by the Spirit of God.

(III) I come now to show the truth of the doctrine.

(A) It is Scriptural. It is a doctrine that the Scripture abounds in. We are there abundantly taught that the saints differ from the ungodly in this, that they have the knowledge of God and of Jesus Christ. I shall mention but a few texts of many: John 14:19, 17:3, I John 3:6, III John 11. And this light and knowledge is always spoken of as immediately given of God, Matt. 11:25-27, II Cor. 4:6. It is said to be by the Spirit of the Lord in II Cor. 3:18. God is spoken of as giving the knowledge of Christ in conversion, as of what before was hidden and unseen. So the Scripture speaks of a knowledge of God's dispensation, and covenant of mercy, and way of grace towards his people, as peculiar to the saints, and given only by God, Psa. 25:14.

The Scripture also teaches that a true and saving belief of the truth of religion is that which arises from such a discovery, John 17:6-8, 12:44-46. There believing in Christ, and spiritually seeing him, are spoken of as running parallel. The apostle Peter mentions it as what gave them (the apostles) good and well-grounded assurance of the truth of the gospel, that they had seen the divine glory of Christ, II Pet. 1:16. The apostle has respect to that visible glory of Christ which they saw in his transfiguration. But if a sight of Christ's outward glory might give a rational assurance of his divinity, why may not an apprehension of his spiritual glory do so too? Doubtless, therefore, he that has had a clear sight of the spiritual glory of Christ may say, "I have not followed cunningly devised fables, but have been an eyewitness of his majesty."

(B) This doctrine is rational. We cannot rationally doubt but that things that are divine, that appertain to the Supreme Being, are vastly different from things that are human. Supposing that God never had spoken to the world, but we had notice that he was about to reveal himself from heaven, and speak to us immediately himself as it were from his own mouth, or that he should give us a book of his own inditing. Would it not be rational to suppose that his speech would be exceeding different from man's speech? Doubtless it would be thought rational to expect this, and unrational to think otherwise, that is, that there should be such an excellency and sublimity in his speech and word, such a stamp of wisdom, holiness, majesty, and other divine perfections, that the word of man should appear mean and base in comparison of it.

It is rational to suppose that this knowledge should be given immediately by God, and not obtained by natural means. Why should not he that made all things still have something immediately to do with the things that he has made? Where lies the great difficulty, if we own the being of a God, and that he created all things out of nothing, of allowing some immediate influence of God on the creation still? How rational it is to suppose that God, however he has left meaner goods and lower gifts to second causes, should reserve this most excellent of all divine communications in his own hands, to be bestowed immediately by himself. It is a kind of emanation of God's beauty, and is related to God as the light is to the sun.

It should be beyond a man's power to obtain this knowledge and light by the mere strength of natural reason, for it is not a thing that belongs to reason, to see the beauty and loveliness of spiritual things. It is not a speculative thing, but depends on the sense of the heart. It is out of reason's providence to perceive the beauty or loveliness of any thing: such a perception does not belong to that faculty. Reason's work is to perceive truth and not excellency.

Conclusion: I will conclude with a brief improvement of what has been said.

This doctrine may lead us to reflect on the goodness of God that a saving evidence of the truth is attainable by persons of mean capacities and advantages, as well as those that are of the greatest parts and learning. Persons with but an ordinary degree of knowledge are capable of being taught by the Spirit of God, as well as learned men. And babes are as capable of knowing these things as the wise and prudent, I Cor. 1:26-27.

This doctrine may well put us upon examining ourselves whether we have ever had this divine light, that has been described, let into our souls. All may hence be earnestly exhorted to seek that spiritual light. It is more excellent than any human learning; it is far more excellent than all the knowledge of the greatest philosophers or statesmen. This knowledge has the most noble object that is or can be, viz. the divine glory and excellency of God and Christ.

This light is such as effectually influences the inclination, and changes the nature of the soul. It assimilates the divine nature, and changes the soul into an image of the same glory that is beheld, II Cor. 3:18. It causes the heart to acquiesce in the revelation of Christ as our Saviour. This light has its fruit in an universal holiness of life. It shows God's worthiness to be obeyed and served.